A Lone Birch
My Artistic Journey

&

Written by
Kate Moynihan

ISBN-13: 978-1984265425
ISBN-10: 1984265423

Library of Congress Control Number: 2018901720

CreateSpace Independent Publishing Platform,
North Charleston, SC

Note from the Author

I may have told the facts of this story differently than others recall, since we each have our own perspective on events. Nevertheless, the telling is true for me, along with the emotions and the lessons I have learned. For narrative purposes, I shortened the timeline of certain events. Aside from references to my immediate family members and iconic businesses, I changed many names.

My hope is you'll grab a cup of coffee and grow with me as I learn to celebrate the imperfect qualities of being human.

Contents

Chapter 1
Thoughts Adrift

The sharp tangy smell of turpentine floats about the art studio and wraps me in a purposeful peacefulness. It is twenty minutes before six – often the best part of my morning. From one of my hefty tubes of oil paint, I squeeze out a mound of Cadmium yellow onto my wood palette.

The color is bold. Yet after 34 years of painting, I am bold as well.

With confidence in my craft, I dip my palette knife into the nearby pool of electric blue I placed there minutes earlier, scrape it across to mingle with the yellow, and mix lush leafy green. Standing, as I usually do when I paint, I eagerly face the crisp-white canvas. The span of canvas is so big that, when I spread my arms wide, I still can't touch both edges. Because I know the amount of time and attention required to finish this piece, my heart embraces the challenge.

I reach for the red. It's so rich it glistens like a garnet. Squishing out a strawberry-size portion, I swirl the palette knife into the vivid green, and the result is a deepened hue to match the pre-dawn darkness lurking outside my studio and shop. December in Holland, Michigan, means the sun won't peek out yet for a couple of hours. The downtown streets will

1

stay dark and empty until Holland's quaint specialty shops – more than a hundred of them – spring open their locks for the bustle of the Christmas shopping season.

However, I don't focus on my shopkeeper duties, such as displaying merchandise or proofing reorders. Instead I'm here early to face my empty canvas with these colors I love. I glance outside as a light snow whirls against the huge storefront windows. Suddenly I catch a glimpse of myself in the reflection. Already smudged with several of my morning's paint choices, the creases on my face reveal that I am no longer a young woman. But I'm here to tell you this: I'm more alive than I was at twenty-five.

Not one to pre-sketch my artistic vision, I scoop up a knife-full of green and pull it across the middle of the canvas as I frame in the background for a large stand of trees to come later. This will be a painting for Adam, the younger of my two sons, still footloose and single in his thirties.

Yesterday, painting this picture was not on my already long to-do list, but that was before a new text vibrated on my first-ever cell phone.

"Do you have any black and white posters for my house?" Adam texted, followed by a smiling emoji.

I purchased this phone to connect more with Adam. He had moved to San Francisco nine years earlier, taking only a backpack on a one-way flight. This fit his carefree nature.

In his childhood, Adam dove into whatever came his way, always curious and spontaneous, like grabbing my old pantyhose to coil around a forked tree branch to create a slingshot. He reminds me of myself.

Throughout his adult life, his contact with me has been erratic. "Oh, Mom, has it really been that long since I called?"

he has said when I fuss about not hearing from him.

Enter technology. I discovered that texting was his pre-ferred mode of contact. So when his never-before-request to me for some artwork came through, I texted back.

"No posters at the gallery anymore. That business moved to the Internet with print-on-demand options. I can paint black and white birch trees, though." I suggested my best-known artistic image.

Adam: "That would be nice."

Me: "Any color?"

"Whatever you think is best. Just put Henry in it."

Henry, his beloved yellow lab, is always at his side. "Got it."

What does it mean for me to create a piece of art for my spirited son? In a word: everything.

As I spread serene blue paint across the canvas for the sky, thoughts turn to my other son, Brian. Unlike his younger brother, Brian wasn't as fond of surprises growing up, always wanting every detail well considered. With concern, he would voice: "What time does the movie actually start, Mom?" To this day he remains perfectly suited in his career as a civil engineer.

For Christmas I will be taking an hour and a half joyride to Battle Creek to spend the holiday with Brian, his wife, Lind-say, and my three grandkids, seven, five and one. Of course, I'd drive anywhere to be able to hug them all!

I count my blessings as I stand in front of the easel on this early morning, yet wonder for a moment about the winding road that brought me here. From deep inside I feel tightness take hold as I think back to who I was when the boys were young. How difficult it can be to think back on some of my early choices. To think about being back there. *Muskegon, Michigan.* A place I began a life-changing journey.

Chapter 2
Tonka

In the spring of 1984, I woke up huddled in a blanket on the hard living room floor of our two-story Colonial. Sometime in the deep of the night, after endless tossing, I'd crawled out of bed leaving Wayne, my husband of nine years, sound asleep as I tiptoed past our preschoolers' rooms and shuffled downstairs. For me, I had another restless, fretful night.

As morning arrived, the rain pelted the window, hindering daylight and my mood. The gloomy weather was my fate this day, so until a break in the storm, I would be stuck indoors in this Colonial that Wayne and I had bought for our growing family. Although a cheerful white siding covered the exterior, brown carpet as dark as the gloomy day dominated the indoors. To lift the dullness, I had painted the walls daffodil, yet today the color felt far from sunny.

From the dining room, the grandfather clock chimed six. A knot formed in my stomach as I gathered up my pillow. Hustling, I knew that in less than thirty minutes, kid mayhem would overtake my day.

Soon enough, it began.

"Mom-mee," Adam's thick and scratchy voice echoed from the top of the stairs.

My typically topsy-turvy day had begun. I wouldn't have a moment to myself for the rest of the day.

"I'm down here," I called to my early rising three-year-old – who also wasn't much of a nap taker. Somehow he survived on less sleep than I did and still woke ready to tackle the day.

Adam scampered down the stairs and bolted toward me for a bear hug. As the little guy squeezed me around the knees, I felt a thrill in my heart and a tension in my stomach all at the same time. His hug lasted all of two seconds; then he shot to the kitchen table, gave one of the heavy oak kitchen chairs a mighty tug and perched on his morning throne. As he plopped his elbows on the table, he waited to be served.

I had no time to consider my own overwhelming feelings. Pushing past the tense stomach, the perplexing feelings, I went into full Mommy mode.

I grabbed a bowl, spoon, milk, and cereal and spread them out on the table. Chin-level to the table top, Adam happily slurped at the swimming rainbow of cereal letters in his bowl as Wayne strolled into the kitchen.

"Hey, there big man," he said, bending over the boy, snatching a kiss while tickling his belly.

Wayne filled the room not so much with his medium-sized frame but with his enthusiasm for the boys. This contentment with the family fit him as well as his button-down shirt and perfectly knotted tie.

In contrast to Wayne, I had my morning hair hastily gathered and tied while my feet shuffled in faded slippers. After I spent half the night on the floor, my tired eyes made me look unsettled for the day ahead. *Why was Wayne fulfilled with our life while I struggled with needing ... what?* I couldn't articulate my confusion. I loved the boys with my

5

entire heart, yet I often labored mentally and emotionally to get through the day.

For all these mixed emotions churning inside, there was no one to blame but myself because when Wayne presented the idea of having a family in 1979, I happily agreed. We'd been married for five years and I had followed Wayne around the country as his career progressed. As a registered nurse, I rotated shifts in five different hospitals in three different states. Repeatedly having low seniority on the work-shift totem pole relegated me to a basic nursing position at each new job. I discovered there wasn't much challenge in checking routine vital signs so I thought being home with children would bring me joy like my mother had found raising my older brother and me.

Wayne gave me a quick peck on the cheek that brought me out of my reverie.

"See everyone tonight at six for dinner," Wayne shouted, blowing kisses back our way until the kitchen door snapped behind him.

The click of that door was like a punch in my gut. In his position as a mechanical engineer, Wayne would be gone for his usual eleven-plus hour workday. Before I had a chance to take in a breath, Brian, our four-year-old, bounded into the room, climbed into his place at the table and stayed his usual quiet self.

"Stay-home?" Adam mumbled through a mouthful of cereal, referring to the nickname that the boys gave non-preschool days. They went to a playgroup two mornings a week.

I nodded yes. It would be another day when the only adult sound would be of my own voice. I tugged open the freezer door to grab a pack of frozen hamburger, but promptly fell into a trance even with the frosty air drifting out.

The *varoom!* of monster trucks speeding across the lino-leum pulled me from my daze. The boys had abandoned breakfast. Adam favored a yellow Tonka truck with massive wheels and front-end loader. He rammed the big rig toward Brian's police cruiser ... but ran over my foot instead. I yelped from the collision, and then felt a throb in my foot that pulsed like the growing ache in my chest.

Tonka. That's it, I thought.

I had found a name to use for the pressure that never ceased to fill my core.

"Sorry, Mom!" Adam squealed. "It was an accident." He looked up, his green eyes wide.

I melted as quickly as I had tensed, and I sank down to give him a loving squeeze. The Tonka-size pressure softened in my chest. Then I caught sight of the list I had clipped to the refrigerator and my spirits lifted a bit more. In an attempt to get more absorbed in my stay-at-home existence, I had taken the boys to the library the day before and checked out several books on kids' activities. With the boys tucked in for the night, I set about planning a more organized itinerary for the three of us. Arts and crafts, in particular, were something with which I was comfortable.

Giving Adam one last squeeze, I rose and announced: "Let's get dressed, boys! We have some special new games to try." I clapped my hands and the boys rallied around my new-found energy, scurrying upstairs, stripping pajamas. I found myself bringing up the rear as my sleepless night had stolen my stamina. I discovered it was easier to scoop up their trail of belongings rather than ask the boys to backtrack to pick up their stuff.

Dressed, we returned to the kitchen table. In record time they whizzed through the new counting and matching numbers game I had prepared last night. Hustling to keep up with their pace, I moved the boys to building pyramids using paper cups. However, just one innocent arm swing by Adam, and Brian's tower toppled. Instantly a scuffle broke out. I brought peace to the disruption by offering the next item on the list, "It's bath time!"

I got quizzical looks from my preschoolers. They'd just gotten dressed only minutes earlier. Once more, we marched up the steps this time toward the tub.

Unfortunately the bath water hadn't even cooled when the boys depleted both cans of Wayne's shaving cream for a foam war and sunk the aluminum-foil boats that I had constructed the night before. As they started splashing a tidal wave onto the bathroom floor, it was time to abort the tub.

"Okay, guys, bath games are over. Let's get dressed." They sprung out of the tub and I shooed them toward their rooms. As I mopped up the floodwaters, I felt my heart sink. We were near the bottom of my activity list! In addition, the grandfather clock struck a warning: It was only seven-fifteen in the morning. It was as if the clock was savoring its numbers instead of ticking them off.

My thoughts swam back to the day before, when I dropped the boys off at preschool and saw other stay-at-home moms happily bouncing off in tennis skirts and leaving me behind. I had no energy to chase around a tennis ball after fetching the boys' stray soccer kicks. *How did they do it? What was I doing wrong that instead of feeling excited about two hours without sticky fingers I felt drained? What was their secret?*

Suddenly Adam charged into the hallway, pulling me

back to the moment. I barricaded his stampede to Brian's room with one arm but dropped wet towels in the process. "Hold up, Adam. You need to help me gather the laundry."

The distraction worked, and he began gathering the wet load. I stepped to the hamper to get the rest of the clothes. Lifting the lid, the sour smell of soiled clothes somehow reminded me of my mother's impressive faithfulness to laundry on Monday, ironing Tuesday, and darning socks Wednesday.

Mom!

I nearly forgot she and Dad were coming to dinner tomorrow evening!

"Change of plans, boys," I said as Brian emerged from his room. "We're going to the grocery store. Grandma is coming tomorrow."

With the kids buckled in their car seats, I felt *Tonka* tighten as Mom's constant homemaker declaration raced through my mind: "It was the happiest time of my life, staying home with you kids. That and being married to your father for thirty-seven years."

My whole life I viewed Mom as a role model, with her happily-ever-after stories. Marriage and motherhood was something women should delight in and be thankful. I shoved the guilt of my dissatisfaction down deep and focused on the task: getting groceries.

Chapter 3

What's Wrong With Me?

Once we returned from the market, the boys sped out to their swing-set to play in the March dampness under gray, ragged clouds.

"Push me, push me!" they squealed.

I dutifully followed and counted the pushes. "One, two, three ..." As their feet kicked merrily in the air, my feeling of isolation surfaced once more, starting with a rumble in my stomach, rising like lava, hot across my chest. Oh, how I yearned to be a good and happy mother and wife.

"Twenty-nine, thirty ..." The swing, going back and forth, yet going nowhere, mimicked my internal struggle.

I pinched the bridge of my nose, squinted and fought against my watering eyes.

I had no idea what to do.

Why didn't I find happiness in all this? In things like sewing, following the simple steps of a pattern like Mom had taught me years ago.

Feeling drained, I gave the boys two final pushes. "Forty-nine ... fifty! That's it!"

The boys scurried off the swings and trotted inside. I flicked on the TV in the adjoining family room. For the moment, Mr. Rogers changing into his cardigan and sneakers while he sang his kindhearted welcome-to-the-neighborhood theme song captivated the boys. As the half-hour children's program provided a distraction, I prepped tacos for our dinner and the lasagna for my parents' visit.

As I worked in the kitchen, muddled thoughts lingered in my head.

What exactly was wrong?

I asked myself that question.

Often.

After all, since I was a young girl I had the same dreams of domestic happiness. *So why did I feel so restless, unsatisfied, and guilty?* I uttered, but in my naïve state the answer did not make it through the layers of my family history. Like my grandmothers and aunts, Mom never considered college or a career. They all married fresh out of high school and coveted raising a family while the men held steady jobs. Their example of marital bliss, my mother's in particular, seemed to block out all other possibilities for me.

One other factor added to my uncertainties. The beginnings of speech, especially for Brian, hadn't come early in the boys' development, yet they had passed every physical checkup since birth at the medical center.

Being a nurse, I knew some toddlers could be late talkers, but I was so concerned that I asked Wayne about it.

"He never complains when we rough house," Wayne said as he sped after the boys.

Yet, during the day, I felt isolated trying to decipher Brian's quiet needs. My insecurity and self-doubts about being a good mother rose.

Finally Wayne and I agreed to have Brian's hearing checked and he passed; a blessing I appreciated.

Squawks rang out as the TV show Mr. Rogers ended. I flicked off the switch and set the boys up with Play-Doh at the kitchen table. As they rolled snakes, I managed to clear the lasagna-prep mess and stow the casserole in the fridge for the next day, ready to cook and serve for dinner at six sharp, not a minute before, not a minute after. Mom's life revolved around my dad, and the evening meal revolved around his punctual clock. Wayne savored the same tradition.

At six on the dot, Wayne breezed in to settle into his spot at the table. The boys mounted their chairs. I served the tacos.

Immediately after dinner, Wayne plopped down on the floor and began building Tinker Toy contraptions with the boys. This was the common practice, with Wayne instantly wrapping himself up in the boys' world. He was as practical and loyal as the daily newspaper, the kind of guy who wanted love everlasting and silver anniversaries and Thanksgivings at big tables. Wayne always seemed so content in his role and I felt guilty for not being like him.

With such thoughts swimming through my head, I realized I wasn't just feeling alone and isolated with the boys, but in my marriage, too. Wayne's needs seemed so different from mine. He genuinely didn't see or feel my struggles. It seemed like we were drifting apart.

My thoughts were confirmed when I remembered one specific Saturday. I had arranged an afternoon babysitter so Wayne and I could delight in the 16-foot sailboat we stowed for one of Wayne's fraternity brothers. In exchange for the storage space, we had free use of the boat. I had invited another couple to sail with us, and I looked forward to the sun tingling my skin, the wind kissing my face, and the water splashing my butt as I hung it over the leeward side when the hull keeled over. While I frolicked, Wayne steered the rudder and kept the vessel stable.

However, as that Saturday morning unfolded, thunder roared and a storm brewed. "We're going to have to cancel sailing," Wayne said.

"How about we keep the babysitter and go to the movie. *Footloose* is showing," I offered, thinking about my hunger to get away from the Colonial and my taste for lively musicals.

"Go to a movie in the afternoon? We can do that some evening when the boys are asleep." He waved me off with his hand and turned to go into the kitchen.

It was as if we were sailing in two different directions, yet I wanted desperately to be happy in my domestic role, like Wayne. Maybe if I just tried harder. Trying harder had always worked in my youth. In high school when I was a cheerleader, I had to try harder, practicing extra solo hours. To get through nursing school, I had to study harder than my roommates did. Therefore, I concluded that if I just tried harder I could be happy like Wayne.

In my efforts to try harder in my marriage and home life, I talked to my neighbor, Wendy, who taught pre-school, thinking she might have some ideas for kids' activities. She showed me a schedule with the day broken into fifty-minute increments. My kids didn't last more than fifteen minutes with one activity, but I was too ashamed to admit that so I shuffled away, withdrawing a bit more.

The long days of being the lone adult in the Colonial had me so overwhelmed I had to try something. The only thing

I knew outside of crafts and being a stay-at-home mom was nursing. The med center had told me I was welcome back any amount of time I could work, but I had never considered it. Until now.

What would my mother think about that idea? She was coming tomorrow so I was about to find out.

Chapter 4
Silence as an Answer

Although Mom was four inches shorter than me, her strong sense of presence made it seem as if she towered above me. With the lasagna dinner and the dishes done, Dad was working a crossword puzzle in the family room. As he completed each answer, he pushed up his bifocals, making his silver handlebar mustache twitch. Meanwhile, all around us, Wayne hunted the boys in an indoor game of Hide 'n' Seek.

The kitchen window was open, yet nothing moved in the stifling air. I tugged a kitchen chair out from the table, sunk into a seat, and invited Mom to join me as I mustered up the confidence to confront her.

Mom settled into her seat, and to me, she appeared ready for action with a helmet of short gray hair, and her everyday armor of a makeup-less face, ready to conquer the day with straightforwardness.

I swallowed to coat my dry throat and pushed out the words: "I'm thinking of going back to nursing for one short shift a week at the family practice office."

"Oh, Kathleen. Why would you want to do a thing like that?"

Like always, she called me Kathleen, my birth name, yet since kindergarten I remembered telling the teacher my name was Kathy, and that stuck with everyone but her.

"You have such a beautiful home here," she added as her eyes scanned the kitchen, taking in appliances she never had: a dishwasher, toaster oven, microwave. Then, in a classic Mom move, one eyebrow lifted – a sign I learned from my youth that she was disappointed in me.

"It's not about the house. It's ..." I paused.

My hesitation was too long. Mom continued. "You girls today want so much more than what your father and I ever had. You have two cars! We just had one. If I wanted to use the Chevy, I had to drive your dad to work struggling with thirty-five minutes of Detroit traffic."

"I remember," I said. "But it's not that I really want more things." I knew right then, no matter how I phrased the next part, Mom wouldn't understand because I, too, didn't understand my restlessness. Somehow I found more words: "Mom, it's just hard to stay home all day."

"Hard?" She leaned forward. "Your dad never changed one diaper, and when I was in bed with the flu he couldn't fix hot dogs for dinner. That was the way my generation was, but not your generation. Wayne is such a big help with the boys. You're so lucky."

"I know, Mom. Wayne is a big help," I said, yet the pressure of *Tonka* in my chest didn't ease.

"What does Wayne say about you going back to work?"

"He said it's okay if that's what I need," I answered, knowing Wayne woke up often to the coldness of my empty side of the bed. He could sense something was off with me even though neither of us understood it.

Mother's mouth dropped open for a second, then snapped closed as her lips drew tight. The tension rose between us. "Have you talked to Carol?" she asked, naming Wayne's mom. "Carol raised five children and she always stayed home just like me."

"Yes," I said. In fact, I'd talked to Carol several times. I repeated the words Carol had shared with me, "The boys will only be young once. The time goes by so quickly."

I had great respect for Carol. At age twenty-four she had four kids under six years old, with the fifth child arriving a few years later. She and Frank, Wayne's dad, had raised them into fine adults.

Included in my conversation with Carol, I asked her about Brian's speech development. There was comfort and support in her voice as she reminded me, "Some kids are naturally quiet, and blossom later."

This proved true when Brian, at three-and-a-half, started preschool. I had hoped being around kids his own age might increase his vocabulary. However, the teachers reported he pulled away more than he joined in, so we decided to wait before sending him again.

Months later Brian returned to the playgroup along with Adam, receiving good reports. I was truly thankful; however, the question of how to get through these eighteen-hour Mom days overpowered me.

I caught sight of my mother's electric blue eyes and their intensity pulled me from my trance.

"Kathleen, you're not thinking clearly." She let out a long sigh. "I thought when you decided to be a nurse you would appreciate motherhood even more."

I dropped my eyes to my lap as the guilt seeped through

me. The paper napkin in my lap became a shredded soggy mess from my sweaty palms. Mom was right. I had chosen nursing.

In one of her classic moves, she got up from her seat and stood as stiff as the straight-back chair.

I felt defeated. The silence hung heavy in the air as I shut down not knowing how to express any more than I had already.

"Well, I can't imagine what more you want. You have it all right here."

With that, Mom left the room – which was her way of ending a conversation. Once Mom gave voice to her opinion, all talk was over. My heart told me this was the only way Mom knew how to help me – giving me advice that had worked for her. I respected that.

Mom showed her support in other ways. When she visited a half dozen times a year, she offered to watch the boys so I could run errands. Before this current trip, Dad had built a wooden storefront. When they arrived, she carried an overflowing bag of pretend cereal boxes, plastic fruit, and a cash register for the boys to play-act.

After our hard conversation about my returning-to-work-idea, Mom and I never mentioned the subject again, and soon the weekend ended.

As my parents headed back to their home in Detroit, I watched the tail lights of their Chevrolet Impala fade away and reflected on how communication with Mom was never our strong suit. Brevity was common with her. During middle school, the day I came to her with great concern regarding what I found in my underwear, she gave me a box of sanitary pads and a booklet on menstruating. In high school we never did have the birds and bees talk. Instead, Mom stated, "If you ever *have* to get married, there'll be no wedding from your father and me."

Without realizing it at the time, I dragged these poor communication skills into my marriage with Wayne.

Chapter 5

A New Discovery

Almost immediately, after that visit by my parents, I started wandering aimlessly. At times in the Colonial, I spaced out and forgot what I was doing in the middle of a simple task like making beds or mopping up a forgotten weeping Popsicle.

Never once did I consider myself sick, physically or mentally. As a registered nurse, I had only learned about extreme anxiety such as schizophrenia or manic-depression. In 1984, the "Just Say No to Drugs" created by Nancy Reagan took root, but the focus was on the American crack cocaine epidemic. Seeing a therapist or popping an anti-depressant never occurred to me.

In my overwhelmed and frustrated state, I reached for the only thing I knew how to do outside the home: be a nurse. Trying to gain focus, I returned to the family practice medical office, working one short shift a week. I discovered that I enjoyed the time away from the house, but it wasn't enough. The conflicting feelings at home continued.

One night when Wayne came downstairs from putting the boys to bed, he flicked on his favorite TV show, *Twilight Zone*, a fantasy that drifted from reality. The haunting music matched the unease in my chest. As the program broke for commercial, I mustered up the courage to ask Wayne a bit more about his contentment with our roles. "Do you ever get bored?"

"Bored?" The shrill of Wayne's word emphasized his surprise. "How could I? There is never a dull moment around here when the boys are awake."

"I know ..." My voice trailed off. "It's just for me, I don't know. The days are long."

"But you went back to work."

"Yeah, I like getting a morning away. That's nice." I knew I wasn't giving Wayne much, but I didn't really know what to give. I couldn't blame Wayne. After all, he met me as the girl who was studying to become a nurse in a twenty-month technical program. Ever since, I had worked as an R.N., a caregiver in a traditional role. It was hard for him to have empathy when he didn't feel the loneliness around us.

As the sinister music of *Twilight Zone* penetrated through me, I moved onto another subject. Recently Wayne's brother-in-law, also a mechanical engineer, had returned for a master's degree in business, saying it was an award-winning combination for advancement. Therefore, I asked Wayne, "Have you thought about going back to college for an MBA?"

"No, I'm happy where I am. I like the routine I have."

As I questioned Wayne about returning to college, it never occurred to me that I might return. I was too lost to realize I was losing my sense of self. Instead the emotional pressure of *Tonka* in my chest deepened. I didn't realize at that moment how I retreated to the communication skills I used with my mother. I shut down, not attempting to voice my inner feelings about which I had very little understanding.

A few days later, as I tugged the boys around another

block in their wagon, I felt the balmy spring breeze brush my face. Although warm, the air chilled me. The small cluster of woods behind our subdivision caught my eye. One particular birch stood struggling to sprout a few leaves. Lightning had struck it and burned its core. Like me, it was alive on the outside but wounded on the inside.

The tree needed to be chopped down.

But what about me?

The next night, the peppery scent of meatloaf hovered as I finished kitchen cleanup while Wayne and the boys made zooming noises with a *Dukes of Hazard* racecar, a souped-up Dodge Charger featured on a popular TV comedy. With my duties done, I thumbed through a stack of mail. A flier from the local art center with a list of classes intrigued me, painting in particular. Then unease swept through me.

One summer my art teacher recommended to my parents that they send me to an art camp. At fifteen, I had been excited to go, only to discover that the precise detail in learning the vanishing point of perspective and the realism in charcoal drawing class pushed my patience as I forced myself to draw with such restrictions.

Standing in the kitchen of the Colonial, staring at the flyer, I wondered if painting would be different. Our only décor to speak of was a group of family photos hanging in the hallway. Wayne thought art was a luxury that didn't fit our budget, but what if I created it myself.

I waved the flier at Wayne as I told him about the once-a-week evening class.

"Maybe with some instructions I could learn to paint. If I'm any good, we might get something to hang on the rest of these walls."

"Painting a picture yourself makes the price right." He tossed a smile my way. "I don't mind chasing these rascals if you want to try." With that he was off wrestling the kids while I reflected on the price-is-right comment from Wayne.

A bit earlier, during one of my home decorating endeavors, I had fallen in love with a porthole-shaped mirror that was perfect for our guest bath off the kitchen. It would complete the nautical theme I had been working on. I told Wayne of my idea and the price of the mirror.

"It's *how* much?"

I repeated the price.

"Wow! That's a lot of money. Besides, the mirror already in there works fine." He spoke of the square of plate glass clipped to the wall with plastic holders. "Kathy, you already spent money on wallpaper."

Even though Wayne's income was substantial to support our life style, saving and conserving were in his nature, and this time he was right. I had bought wallpaper. Nevertheless, I really liked that mirror – round with a thick frame, knobs like a real porthole with rope trim. Instead of "talking" about how we could budget the mirror or waiting several months to ask to receive it as a May birthday gift, I just snapped my mouth shut.

Along with my poor communication skills, I inherited a portion of French stubbornness. From then on, I just started writing my check at the grocery store for ten dollars more and stashing the money aside to buy the things I wanted. At the time, I couldn't see how my immature and self-centered ways, along with our different perspectives on budgeting for home décor, divided Wayne and me.

Using the silent treatment kept harmony with Wayne's

plan-every-detail personality, but unknowingly, it put a greater gap between us, making me feel isolated not only in the Colonial, but in our marriage, too.

As the boys zipped by me, speeding their racecars through the kitchen, I caught sight of Wayne's shoes in the corner boot tray, paired squarely aligned side by side as if the shoes were snapping to attention. When I met him at nineteen, I thought it was Wayne who lit up the world around me. Thinking back decades later, I became aware that the spontaneous, infectious vibe from his Greek fraternity was what made the chills dance up my spine, not Wayne's structured safety-net of routines. Yet, at the moment, I couldn't comprehend it all.

Six days later I headed to art class, leaving all three boys building Lego towers with Wayne's nose buried deep into the picture-maps of directions, exactly following step one, step two . . .

I had crossed over twenty-nine when my first watercolor lesson captivated me. The hour-long class whizzed by. I discovered that this new medium offered me a challenge I'd never had before. The colors radiated richer than the spring greens that sprang outside the classroom window. On the wet paper, the rain-forest green I mixed soon separated: blue went one way, yellow-green flowed another. They spilled wherever they wanted to go!

These unexpected surprises in watercolor were completely different from all the crafts I had tried where I simply repeated the same steps over and over. I fell in love with the freedom and spontaneity of the paints. What joy to discover the complexity of watercolor! For the first time since I could remember, I felt inspired, challenged, and eager for more.

My painting hobby, as Wayne, my mom, and even me,

called it, as I never imagined anything beyond a homemaker role in my life, started to fill a bit of that dark *Tonka* ache in my chest. However, returning part time to the medical office pushed me into an old pattern I didn't fully recognize.

Chapter 6
If I had Only Known

His name was Robert.

He was tall, dark-haired, handsome. A doctor in the medical office where I worked.

I had returned to nursing one short shift a week, and ignored the fact that my head lifted each time this man waltzed into the room. *Just shrug off this distraction. Chalk it up to his ability to fill a room with his personality. You're just here to get a break from too much stay-home time.* Therefore, I just focused on my work.

Then, unexpectedly, Dr. R. strolled down the hall wearing a light blue lab coat instead of the traditional crisp white one. He rapped on a patient door and disappeared inside, but his *blue* coat didn't disappear from my thoughts. Instantly my mind raced back to that memorable day when I first met him five years earlier wearing a *blue* lab coat. Back then, in 1979, I was a twenty-five year old gal who had joined his office because I wanted to leave the grueling night-and-day rotation of hospital shifts. Day jobs were hard to find for a young nurse.

On that first day of training at the medical office, while I shadowed my co-worker, Dr. R strolled into the treatment room. I felt my breath hitch, caught off guard on two counts: First, I had only seen doctors wear white lab coats, not blue, and secondly, by his youthful appearance. He couldn't have been more than a handful of years older than me, whereas the other physicians in the group were more like my dad's age.

"This is Kathy, our new nurse," my coworker introduced me that first day.

The doctor stepped toward me. There was magnetism to his pace and an air of confidence that simply radiated – as powerful to me as the nuclear explosion that had recently occurred at Three-Mile Island in Pennsylvania.

"I'm Dr. R," he said, flashing a smile so smooth that it could soothe a crying baby.

Awestruck, I stared at the broad shoulders under that blue lab coat, a blue that matched his mystical eyes. I felt my heart pulse rapidly in my neck. *He's so tall with such grace. Wait. Where do these thoughts come from? I'm a married woman! He's a doctor! In addition, married, too. With children, I hear!*

I slapped on a small smile to mask the foolish, schoolgirl thoughts that raced through my mind. Somehow I uttered a professional response. With my composure gathered, I stepped back and watched him flawlessly suture a gaping wound on a plumber.

By the end of my first day, I realized that the charismatic Dr. R talked to everyone with warmth and compassion. His enthusiasm was contagious, whether he spoke to a shuffling 87 year-old lady, an attorney in a $400-suit, or Val who answered the phones. The common theme of his interactions was that whenever he spoke, all heads turned his way.

After working at the med center for a month, one late afternoon, after we had hustled to treat an endless number of patients due to a hectic flu season, Dr. R uncorked a bottle of wine. The entire team kicked up their feet and had a sip together. Never before in my years of nursing had a doctor mixed with staff. In school they taught us to serve them as masters.

With a breezy smile, he said to the group, "The musical production of *Evita* is playing at the Shubert Theater in Chicago."

Silently I felt equal parts uneducated and artless as I sat enthralled, concentrating on his superior knowledge of theater and opera. There had always been a bit of mystery to him as he radiated his infectious energy.

"Listen to this recording sometime," he said to us, holding out a vinyl record album of *Evita* he had brought into the office. "It's one of my favorites." He offered the music to the office group, but I was the one to reach for it. I had always enjoyed the old musicals of Fred Astaire and Bing Crosby. Every Christmas I checked *TV Guide* for *Holiday Inn* so I wouldn't miss the annual re-run showing.

Back at our Colonial, as I did household cleanup, the elegant Andrew Lloyd Webber vocals of *Evita* floated to my ears, wrapped around me, and carried me off in another world. When Wayne heard the light operatic music, he said, "It's nothing like Alice Cooper." He chuckled as he mentioned his favorite shock-rocker.

Dr. R. shared more of his love for opera. I listened to *Pirates of Penzance* and *Madam Butterfly* and more. As time continued to unfold, I listened to the *Tale of Genji* while my first baby bump began to protrude from my belly. When

Brian was born, I left the office to stay home. Fifteen months later, Adam arrived.

Abruptly, I heard the latch click of a patient-room door open. I lifted my head and the once-again sight of Dr. R's blue lab coat brought me back to the present, snapping away all thoughts of my past. As he came down the medical office hallway, his blue eyes seemed even brighter sparkling against his blue coat. He stopped next to me and said, "I brought some classical music for you to try. Follow me to my office."

There was a gentle tease to his voice, and it tickled up my spine. I trailed behind. In his office he handed me the soundtrack to *Amadeus.*

"I haven't seen the movie yet," I said, "but I can't wait to hear this soundtrack. It recently won a Grammy Award." I felt breathless and giddy about Dr. R sharing this new release with me, a nurse in the office.

Amadeus, a musical fictional biography of Mozart, had debuted last month, and when I had mentioned one day to Wayne about maybe going to see the film, he said, "Sure, we can go sometime." His tone was supportive, but he quickly changed the subject. "I'm taking the boys to the park to play on the slides. We'll be back in an hour."

Accurately, I think, I took his response as lack of interest in the movie and never asked again to go. Without realizing it, once more I had reverted to the communication "nonskill" that I had learned: silence. The gap between Wayne and me widened.

Back in the Colonial, while five-year-old Brian and four-year old Adam raced about, I played Mozart's soothing music, letting it flow into my soul. The calming melodies helped ease the throb of *Tonka* pressing in my chest.

For a week I let the notes float all around me. After having my fill, I returned the album to Dr. R. When I walked into his office, record in hand, he raised his head and I met his gaze. Those eyes invited me in so I offered more. "Thanks for sharing this. Just recently I started taking a watercolor class, and I especially enjoyed listening to this while I painted."

"I'll bet it helped with the creativity." He graced me with a smile.

Encouraged by that smile, I went on, "There's a lot to learn about watercolors, and I'm enjoying the challenge."

"Challenges are great. You should take another class and learn more."

Just then, the office intercom buzzed, and he picked up the line. I let myself out and realized I wore a smile of my own. Until that moment, all I heard from others for encouragement was how wonderful it was to raise small children. At the time, Dr. R seemed to be the only person to understand that I could have interests outside of the two boys.

Months passed, and the oppressive August sun sizzled outside, yet even the medical office air conditioning did little to chill the spark and heat I felt whenever I sensed someone behind me ... because I *knew* it was Dr. R. I could feel his presence, an intensity that trailed wherever he went.

"I finished hospital rounds early so I went to the art fair going on downtown," he said. "And look what I bought!" He hefted a framed watercolor bursting with a vivid scene of blueberries ripe on the bush, ready to fall or perhaps be picked.

My mouth dropped in awe of the beauty of the watercolor.

Watching a grin rise at the corners of his mouth, I felt this invisible thread stretch between us, connecting us. We had something in common, clearly, even if it was just an affinity to blue fruit on a piece of white paper.

Yet, it was more than that.

Dr. R was different from any other man I had known. Strikingly different.

Finally I found my voice: "Oh! I wish I painted that well."

"I bet you do, or you certainly can. You should bring in some of your pieces for me to see."

At that very notion of someone wanting to see my art, I raised my gaze from the painting to his eyes, and they fixed on me. I saw compassion there, making me feel comfortable to share more. "Well, you should know that during my first critique, the instructor pointed to one area in the work, saying it was a nice painting ..."

He interrupted me. "See? I told you!"

"No, wait, I didn't finish. The nice area was the size of a quarter!"

We laughed at the same time.

"Well, I'd still like to see the work that has you so excited."

Chapter 7

At First, Just a Hobby

My attempts at art were stacked on a Formica table tucked between the washing machine and the boys' costume box in the basement. I shuffled through the jumble of work, feeling just as jumbled on the inside. *Really? Someone actually wanted to see these!*

The next week I toted some of my work to the office.

Later in the day, when we had a break, Dr. R scanned the stack and his lips quickly rose into a full smile. "Alluring," he said. "I like them."

I felt a rush of a blush.

"You should sell some of these," he suggested.

I glanced away, feeling the heat on my cheeks creep farther across my face.

"No, really, I bet they'd sell," he persisted.

Not only did Dr. R encourage me that day, but the next week. And the next.

Easing out of summer, September arrived with a flicker of hope from Dr. R's persistent interest in my work. Eventually, I mustered enough confidence to tell Wayne about trying to sell some of the paintings.

"Where would you do that?" Wayne asked.

"There's a co-op gallery in town," I said, telling him about the Robin Gallery that my watercolor instructor, Shirley Calmworth, had mentioned. I was thrilled at the thought of actually showing in a gallery.

"Does it cost anything to join?"

"They take a percentage of the sales, and we work a few hours in the gallery ourselves."

The questions from Wayne poured out.

"What percent do they take?

"How many pieces do you give them?"

"Are you assigned a specific shift to work?"

"Do you work a certain day?"

My husband preferred to know all the details about things, whereas I was ready to jump ahead! *There was a possibility I would be in a real gallery!* That was all I knew and, for me, which was all I needed to know.

"I haven't learned about the specifics, but I'd like to find out more about it. I can schedule an interview while the boys are at school."

"Kathy, I thought you were painting to make a piece for the house. You know … a hobby. You really think you want to try and sell your work?"

"Well, I've discovered that it's really challenging, and my instructor thinks I'm good enough." I skipped Robert's comments, persuading myself that Wayne wouldn't care about that detail. Only later would I realize this omission constituted the starting point of suppressing the feelings I began to have for Robert. Instead, I took the first step to exhibiting my artwork by saying, "Well, I'd like to at least check out the details of the gallery."

"I guess that can't hurt anything," said Wayne.

One day about a week later, I parked our sub-compact hatchback Chevette in front of a two-story, Victorian-style home in the historic district of town. A florist occupied the main floor; the art gallery I was visiting occupied the second level. The day was cool, quiet, serene – a stark contrast to my internal chaos of nerves. I stepped inside the front door, the art portfolio clutched to my chest. The floral shop bloomed with the sweet scent of lilies and roses. Ignoring the heavy aromas, I looked about and saw a sign for the gallery upstairs.

I headed over but found myself lingering on the stairwell to gawk at the artworks hanging there, paying particular attention to the soft, almost elusive watercolor washes. I spotted a remarkable complex painting of a pint of peaches brimming with color, nestled among twisting vines of summer squash and watermelons. Its freshness sang off the paper with expertise, especially the background painted full of shadowy depth. The art seemed years beyond my hobby capability. *Was I good enough to join this elite group?*

Next to a large desk in the gallery office, I sat at the edge of my office chair as three ladies looked back and forth at the four watercolors I had brought. Three were of single flowers floating on the white paper, leaving the background primarily blank. On the fourth image, I had painted a barn balanced between loose watercolor washes insinuating sky and fields. Beginner stuff, truth be told.

The ladies gave a round of nods. One spoke up. "These are simple, yet you maintain freshness. We would be delighted to have you be part of our gallery."

I wanted to fly out of my chair! This acceptance felt better than any gift I had ever received!

Regarding details of the gallery business, I forced myself

One of my first watercolors, 1984

to sit still and pay attention in order to answer Wayne's questions. Once through the specifics, I bounced down the stairs and frolicked my way back to the Chevette. With thirty minutes to spare before I had to pick up the boys, I steered the hatchback to the home of Shirley, my watercolor instructor, to share my good news.

Earlier, when my weekly adult education classes ended, Shirley had invited me to bring in paintings for her to critique. I felt fortunate to have someone with her level of expertise taking time for me. I had gone to her home twice before. On my last visit, she shared with me that she had a request from a customer to purchase one of her paintings, but the art needed mailing. "I told him 'no,' however."

I gasped. I wanted to blurt out: "That's great! What an honor!" Minding my manners, I stayed quiet. Shirley never rushed, not even in conversation.

Then she offered her reason. "It's a lot of trouble to pack up art."

When I pulled into Shirley's driveway after my exciting gallery visit, her ten-year-old Rambler in the driveway revealed she was almost certainly inside her simple, single-story ranch. Shirley was an exquisite painter, having taken classes with some of the finest masters. I always believed she could have been a nationally recognized artist, but Shirley was happy in her no-frills ranch, sneakers, and experimenting with watercolors in between baking a pineapple-glaze ham hock for her family.

I rapped a robust knock, Shirley answered the door, and I shared my news of the Robin Gallery acceptance. She blossomed into a broad smile and hugged me. "Congratulations! Honestly, I knew they would. You're very talented!" I thanked her for all of her encouragement and valuable instruction, then left to fetch the boys.

That night I shared my happy news with Wayne: "They accepted me! I can have four or five framed paintings on the wall at a time."

"Framed art? How do you get that?"

"I can order inexpensive metal frames. I screw the corners together myself from the Cheap Joe's catalog where I buy my paint supplies. You might remember that Shirley taught all of us in the class how to use a hand-held mat cutter."

Wayne asked a litany of other questions, finishing up with, "What if the framed art doesn't sell? What do you do with it?"

"Well, maybe we could give some as gifts to your family." In past Christmases I had made cornhusk wreaths, macramé snowflake ornaments and other crafts.

Wayne nodded. "I suppose my sisters would like art. My mom probably, too."

That was all the encouragement I needed. In the basement I swung a paintbrush during the boys' two school mornings a week. When I was on the schedule, I practically skipped to my half-day shift per month at the gallery.

On painting mornings I joyfully let the watercolors flow from my corner studio space. In the distance I heard the nearby high school marching band practice, all the while feeling as lively as the high notes of the trumpets.

I also listened to an internal medley of trepidations: *Would people like my work?*

Sure, the gallery judging committee understood the complexity of watercolor, but would a general audience? Would they laugh at my simple skill level?

Chapter 8
The Start of it All

It was a rain-beating-on-the roof, stay-indoors day with the boys, and I was crawling on all fours laying down two parallel strips of removable painter's tape to define a racetrack loop through the kitchen, living room and dining room. My rainy day crew had been pinballing from one activity to another. The racetrack fun took a dark turn, though. Without warning, I glanced up just in time to see Adam arch his arm back and fire a Matchbox toy car at Brian. The car hit him dead center in the forehead; he shrieked so loud my ears rang. Blood gushed. I snatched a dishtowel, grabbed Brian in my arms, held the cloth to the wound, and rocked him to ease his angst. Adam withered from afar.

"It's alright. It's alright." I hadn't seen enough of the incident to know who provoked whom, so I focused on the first aid. Brian's wound was too deep for a butterfly Band-Aid to pull the puncture together.

After Brian's wails settled, I said, "We need to have a doctor look at this. For now I'll wrap you up like a mummy, okay?" I untwisted a gauze roll around his head to keep a pressure dressing in place. "Let's get in the car, boys. They'll take good care of you, Brian, when we get to my med center."

When we got to the doctor's office, the girls coddled Adam while Brian and I hustled into the treatment room. One of my nursing co-workers prepared Brian for his upcoming stitches and then left. A minute later the attending physician on duty came in. It was Dr. R.

"Another ordinary day at school?" he asked Brian, scooting closer on a rolling stool and whispering more small talk into my son's ear as a way of comforting him. Dr. R's tone of voice was smooth, almost a purr. Standard Dr. R charm, he pulled in the patient like a people magnet.

Brian's breathing steadied and his tension noticeably eased under this man's spell.

As the room filled with the smell of antiseptic, Dr. R worked efficiently, coaxing Brian through each step. In only minutes the sutures were in place and Brian was sitting up straight, head high, wearing his stitches like a badge of honor.

With the patient doing well, Dr. R's eyes fixed on mine.

Maybe his look of concern was because of Brian's accident.

Maybe it was worry over my bloodshot eyes from my string of sleepless nights.

Maybe it was a general empathy for me, considering that Adam had burst through the door and the brothers instantly argued about who should get the root beer sucker or the strawberry sucker.

Whatever the reason, something at that time deepened between Dr. R and me.

As autumn progressed, Dr. R and I explored interests we had never taken time to discuss before ... travel ... theater ... trading tidbits of our lives. He even listened to the parts about me that were difficult to admit.

"Watercolor seems to be my only inspiration. I'm struggling with being at home with the boys," I said, spilling truths about myself that I usually kept hidden. "It's lonely and empty."

"Maybe you should take an extra day to paint. Get a sitter for yourself."

I looked at Dr. R as if he were speaking a foreign tongue. Wayne would never understand that I wanted a babysitter just so I could paint more. He watched the kids when I needed to paint.

Dr. R moved closer and gave my shoulders a gentle pat. "Embrace who you really are, Kathy. Your true self. Not just the talents but the flaws, weaknesses, all of it. You be you."

At this very complicated time in my young years, he seemed to be the only person who understood me, who didn't judge me.

By November Dr. R had become Robert to me. His pleasing tenor tones lulled me into a daydream state that I didn't want to leave even when I pressed myself about the situation: *He's married!* I had met his wife, Janet. For their kids' annual checkups, she'd bustle into the office with the children in tow. Although I had known Robert for seven years, more recently Wayne and I attended several large social gatherings with Janet and Robert.

Despite all perspective I should have had about the situation, my self-coaching that he was married and off-limits flew away like the autumn leaves in a whirlwind. He was supremely self-assured and, given my low self-esteem, I found that quality seductive. He began taking over my thoughts. I wasn't proud of it; I should have known better, but I couldn't stop it. One look in those eyes and better judgment be damned. I fooled myself into thinking it was a coincident that we were scheduled to work more shifts together, even though I was the one who set the nurses' calendar.

As the autumn days grew shorter, our conversations grew longer as he asked me to stroll down the block and join him for lunch. I convinced myself he did that just to break up his day. There wasn't any harm; we just talked ... and laughed.

January rang in the new year and our building Christmas party. After being home all day with our sons, I was looking forward to this special evening out. Wayne, though, had no interest in the party, preferring to toss some midwinter Nerf hoops indoors with the boys.

At the party the pharmacist from upstairs played bartender. I accepted a glass of hot cinnamon cider and then sipped my way through the mundane, usual adult conversations about "How are the kids?" and "Any special plans for the new year?"

I took one last sip of my simmered brew and was getting ready to leave when Robert strolled in. During the seven years I had worked at the medical office complex, he had never shown up before. His eyes twinkled brighter than Santa Claus. Then he did something I couldn't believe. He beckoned me with a sly grin and the crook of a single finger. The magnetic pull summoned me and propelled me to his side. He leaned over and crooned in my ear, his voice so low only I could hear: "I was hoping you'd be here."

Me? My old-fashioned belief that doctors surpassed the ranks of nurses made my heart beat faster at the notion that he actually came to see me!

"Let's step away from here."

As Robert took me by the elbow and ushered me toward

the door, my brain waged a small battle over whether I should continue, or turn around and go back to the party. Losing that battle, I found myself stepping into his office and not even remembering our walk down two flights of stairs and a long corridor. Once we were alone, Robert clicked on a lamp. I'd never been in his office at night. In the soft amber lamplight, Robert touched my cheek with his fingertips. A hundred tingles traveled down my spine. I don't know how long we stood there in the first embrace of our lives until his lips brushed mine. I do know that when the kiss ended, my confusion didn't.

I separated from our embrace and excused myself to slip into the bathroom. Thoughts of Wayne flashed through my mind, and I felt my cheeks heat up with guilt.

Unaware of how much time had passed, I heard a soft rap on the door.

"Are you okay?" A sense of urgency filled Robert's voice.

His concern twisted my insides.

The pull to him was so strong even when I didn't want to feel it.

Another soft tap echoed on the door.

"I'll be right out."

I reached for the doorknob and discovered it was cold in my sweaty palm. Taking a deep breath to steady my racing heart, I tugged the door open.

As I came out into the hallway, our eyes locked for a couple of beats and then Robert lowered his gaze. The air felt thick with unsaid words.

He turned back to the small office. In the amber light he paced. "I don't know if I'm ready for this," he said.

His words were an abrupt change considering that, only

moments earlier, he had been holding me in his arms. *Maybe he meant straying from his marriage? Because his heart was loyal to his family?* I didn't get a chance to ask.

"Maybe we should just go home," he said.

I nodded yes, although the rest of me stood frozen, unable to feel my feet beneath me.

He helped me into my coat and placed a gentle hand on my shoulder. That was all, though, just a gentle touch. Then he buttoned his overcoat, tugged up his collar, and steered me to the door. Outside, a hearty gust of wind blew loose snow sideways and slammed freezing flakes into our faces. It made for a quick goodbye – truly an actual blessing in disguise – as my ying-yang emotions tugged at me for my entire drive home.

In all those swirling thoughts, my better judgment told me this: *The smart thing would be to quit the job. You're asking for trouble!*

My foolish heart, of course, refused to listen.

I was already hooked on Robert's ability to ease the loneliness from my predictable days. He was like a drug, and I had become dependent on his attention. I didn't want to admit the truth, but I knew I would go back for more.

Chapter 9
Wayward Feelings

When I pulled up to the Colonial, post party, it didn't look like confinement, but it still whispered the word to me from somewhere deep inside. The darkened windows told me the kids were asleep upstairs, and Wayne was in the back of the house downstairs. As I came through the door, he was standing in the kitchen, holding a cup waiting for the coffee pot to finish percolating.

"Hey," he greeted me without looking up.

While hanging my coat in the closet, my head spun with thoughts of what just happened with Robert.

"Did you have a good time?" he called out as I stood at the closet.

"It was fine."

What else could I say? Then, without realizing it, I began pacing in tight circles of worry trying to catch my breath. Wayne didn't notice; his eyes focused on the bubbling glass knob on top of the percolator. He didn't see me percolating right nearby; he didn't think to pull me to safety. He didn't feel the ground beneath us tremble and shift. Sadly, I didn't tell him either. As I had done so often with my mother, I switched the subject instead of confronting my confusion.

"How was your night with the boys?"

"Great!" The bubbling of the coffee pot slowed so Wayne grabbed the handle to pour a cup while telling about the boys: "I ... am ... a ... robot," he said in a silly mechanical voice.

"So you played Transformers," I surmised, knowing very well about one of the boys' favorite toys. They were the semi-trucks that twisted and turned into Titan super action figures.

"Do you want a cup of coffee?" he asked with all eyes on his mug as he poured the black brew.

"No, thanks." Like a coward, I slunk down the hall. "I'm going to take a bath." Avoidance was easier than facing the truth.

"Sure thing," Wayne said, knowing it was a nightly ritual for me.

I escaped to the tub as I had for the past few years each evening. It had become my place to hide. This time I convinced myself that slinking off to take a bath gave me time to think of what to do next. Letting the soothing water seep around me, I convinced myself things would return to normal with Robert and me simply talking. That meant it was safe to keep my job.

Slowly the minutes clicked off the clock; Saturday finally turned to Sunday and, at last, to the end of the work week when Robert and I had a shift together. He cornered me in the back hallway. "I think we should keep some distance and be professional," he whispered.

I shouldn't have been surprised. After the kiss, he said he didn't know if he was ready.

Ready for what? To explore the feelings he had for me?

For that entire previous week, I interpreted his words a

45

thousand different ways as I wrestled with my own moral confusion. I tried to convince myself we could stay friends, and I could salvage Robert's supportive friendship to help me cope. Now, as he made it clear he wanted to keep some distance from me, I realized I'd become dependent on him. He had pushed me to try new things. He'd encouraged me to stretch myself. He was the stuff that brought my dreams alive, and at the thought of losing him, I felt panic.

The pause that followed felt weighted with things that begged to be said, but he dropped his gaze and walked away.

I stayed there in the hallway, unable to move.

"Are you okay?" a passing co-worker asked. "Your face is red."

"I just need some water."

The distraction of breaking and filling the ice cube trays gave me enough time to pull myself together and push down the overwhelming feelings.

Through the rest of the morning, I avoided eye contact with Robert, afraid my dam of emotions would burst.

Then, at lunchtime, I felt a nudge on my elbow. "Grab your coat," said the voice I knew so well. "Let's take a walk outside."

I wasn't sure I had the strength to hear him out. But I didn't have the strength to stay away, either. I followed his lead, shoving my hands in my pockets against the bite of the thirty-degree winter day.

Robert bent to the cold, too, but then glanced around the empty walk and leaned in closer. "Janet and I are finished," he said, speaking of his wife.

These words about his marriage sent a jolt through me. I never expected something so abrupt. My thoughts were almost a roar in my ears, but the only real sound around us was the crunching of snow as car tires rushed by on the street.

Finally, he spoke again. "We've been drifting apart for a while, even did some marriage counseling. She thinks it's time to separate, and I agree. I came to the Christmas party because I wanted to see you. But maybe that was a mistake." His eyes held mine, and he absentmindedly ran a hand through his hair. "I don't want to influence you when things are changing so quickly for me. That's why I think it's best we stay professional."

I tried to absorb the context of what he was saying and what he was not saying. If I heard correctly, this was Janet's idea and he agreed. *Yet how did he really feel about it?*

"I'll be moving into a condo in February. Janet is staying in the house with the kids. It'll take some getting used to, but I think I'll like my new freedom."

It was so much information to process. I was sure I missed some of what he said. Yet I was certain he would now be more "available."

But how did he actually feel about me?

Then reality brought me back: I was a married woman with children.

Why was I even thinking like this?

Had my heart not been in my throat, and had I not been trying to focus through the overload of our emotions, I would have spoken. The news shocked me, and the only way I survived was to breathe my way through that moment. And then the next. And then each second that hung between us.

"We better get back inside." He guided my arm and I shuffled trance-like.

The rest of the day, I had a loud hum in my head as I tried

to focus on work. I wanted to ask Robert a hundred questions, but I was too overwhelmed to ask even one. Somehow I got through my shift. If we said goodbye, I don't remember.

My sleepless nights increased.

Due to a co-worker's need to change a shift at the office, two weeks passed before I had a shift alongside Robert. I arrived with a racing heart, still unsure what I would say to him. I busied myself with opening duties and shared responsibilities with another nurse in our work station.

Shortly, Robert entered the doorway and straddled its wide frame with his open arms as the morning rays lit him from behind. His mesmerizing aura turned my head.

He said a soft hello and good morning to the two of us. My eyes met his, but our equilibrium felt off.

Later, when I was alone in the hallway, a hint of his musky scent arose from behind me. "You look like *you're* the one going through a divorce," Robert whispered observantly. He must have noticed the dark circles under my eyes.

He waited for an answer, but all I had were questions. I tried rolling all my unanswered thoughts into one. "Should I be?"

"Maybe you and Wayne should try counseling?"

That was the last concept I expected from Robert. Deep inside I hoped my question would tell me more about his new freedom. Shamefully, I felt jealous of this man who was "suddenly available," while I was married with conflicting feelings about my home life. What will happen if he fell in love with someone else? A sour taste filled my mouth. Could I stand aside and let Robert move on with his "single status" without me? The bitterness in my throat swelled as Robert's words scrambled my brain: *Maybe you and Wayne should try counseling.* He was already moving on without me! My chest constricted. I tried to draw a breath that would reassure me that I was okay; instead, I felt my head go light.

"Do you need to sit down?" he asked.

I nodded and turned away, trying to hide from my co-workers. We stepped into the treatment room and I steadied myself in a chair. With uncertainty, I gazed into his eyes. They felt as chilly as the layer of frost etched on the room's only window. A cold jolt ran through me.

Counseling? Was he really rejecting me after all those months that we talked, laughed, joked? Was it my imagination that he enjoyed it, too? And that kiss?

Demoralized with worry that I might lose him, I managed to push out a few words of relevant conversation. "How did your move go? Do you like your freedom?"

"The move is behind me. It was a big step. But this new life is so ..." His voice trailed off and he looked up to the window. "I'm not sure what I'm feeling."

I had my answer.

A biting taste of jealousy turned into a stab in the chest as a feeling of rejection overpowered it. This crushed my confidence, leading me to believe I had lost Robert – the one person who understood my difficulties and me.

The intercom buzzed for him. An emergency pulled Robert away, and we never had a chance to talk more that day. When he left, he took a piece of my heart that I was certain he didn't know he had.

Thoughts of Robert plagued me every minute. Sometime during the next several days of being wounded with emotions, I ventured into new territory.

Chapter 10
Stunned

The sleepless nights had mounted to a point where my head was in a fog most of the time. I rearranged the disgrace of being unhappy as a stay-at-home mom to make room for the guilt of having thoughts outside of Wayne. I dragged myself through kitchen duties, discovering I didn't have enough energy to scrub the crusty remains of boiled-over spaghetti sauce on the stovetop. Instead, I swept dust bunnies under the rug.

I had to do something. Trying a variety of crafts had been my number-one answer for years, but outside of watercolors now, the hobbies didn't ease the *Tonka* in my chest. Only Robert could do that with his words of encouragement. *Would he have time for me as his new life flourished?* Insecurities flooded me.

One evening as darkness draped the Colonial, Wayne came down from his routine of putting the kids to bed and I followed him to talk. Parking himself at the kitchen table, he picked up a water softener agreement to contemplate the fine print of the deal.

Shifting into a nearby chair at the table, I blurted out my words, "I need some help."

"Sure, what kind?"

I licked my dry lips and took a deep breath, knowing Wayne probably thought I needed him to fix a leaky faucet or change the oil in the Chevette.

"I'm not sleeping, Wayne. I don't understand why, but this life isn't enough for me," I divulged, letting one arm circle around the room and then wave toward the ceiling, indicating the entire house.

His mouth dropped open. The silence was deafening.

I chewed my lip, and then pressed on, knowing I had blind-sided Wayne. I rambled on about my home frustrations, and he obviously had no idea how to comprehend it all.

After all ...

Wayne was thriving,

I was barely surviving.

Wayne was the perfect parent,

I was the flawed one.

Wayne was loyal,

I was drifting.

When I asked about seeking counseling, he rubbed his forehead as his brow furrowed. "If that's what you need," he said.

I never uttered a word about my feelings for Robert. Too ashamed of my dependency on a man outside my marriage, I convinced myself it wasn't necessary to mention one word of my betrayal to Wayne because Robert was moving on with his life. I was left behind, trying to pick up the pieces of the mess I had made of my life.

Calling to schedule a counseling appointment, I was encouraged that the first session was to be as a couple. Wayne agreed to come. A few days later, I sat in the counselor's office sharing my guilt as Wayne sat quietly beside me. "Everyone thinks I should be so happy with my life. Two healthy kids, a loyal husband. So why do I feel alone in that house?" My voice broke off and I turned away, ashamed about my selfishness for being unhappy with what I had.

"How do you feel?" the counselor asked Wayne.

Wayne's hands had been in his lap. He opened them, palms up, indicating he didn't have a clue, probably still overwhelmed by my request for counseling. "I thought things were fine."

I felt my shoulders hunch and curl inward as I withdrew in shame. This was so hard for me. I had many more questions in my head about what was wrong with me than answers. *Where did I begin*? Instead all I could utter was what I understood. "Wayne is great with the boys. He can't get enough of them."

A smile spread across Wayne's face. "It's true. I can't get enough, even though they're a lot of work. Typical kids. They bicker, they cry, don't want to go to bed at night."

I nodded in agreement, and then hung my head not uttering a word.

The counselor interjected, "Would you mind if I talk to each of you separately?"

When I was alone with the counselor, I kept my eyes in my lap, too humiliated to look elsewhere.

"What do you think you need?" the counselor asked.

I pushed out a few words, not knowing if they made any sense. I babbled about my mounting sense of inadequacies in my marital and parental roles. Then I stumbled on other words, sharing the loneliness I felt while alone with the boys, yet how my mom, Wayne and others could embrace every moment. I considered touching on the alluring quality that I found in Robert, but I wasn't sure I knew the truth about that. The words sat right there on the tip of my tongue, but I wasn't strong enough to spit out any more. I had already exposed my hurting heart and guilt for being a bad mother.

It continued like this for half an hour, the counselor always answering with another question.

Once our individual sessions concluded, the counselor suggested scheduling another set of separate sessions.

"If you think it might help," Wayne said in response to the counselor, though he had turned to me.

"I'd like to try," I said, hoping I might learn what was wrong with me.

As we rode home, sullenness crawled into every corner of the car. I felt weighted down, unsure of where I stood with anything.

Finally Wayne spoke up, "Kathy, do you think the counselor can help? I'm not sure what we're fixing."

At that moment guilt slapped me in the face for being ungrateful about Wayne's provisions, and the pull that Robert had on me.

Somehow I convinced myself that if Robert understood my motherhood frustrations, maybe counseling could help me understand those frustrations, too, and then it could help Wayne and me. "I think I need fixing," I said, too confused to offer more.

We entered the house, and without taking his coat off, Wayne sat on the floor to wrestle with the boys. I didn't have any emotional fortitude left so I shoved everything deep down where I didn't have to think about it. The house felt small, even with 3,500 square feet. I slunk to the bathtub

Kate Moynihan

– my place to escape – sliding low to let the hot water rush around me, trying to ease the noise in my head.

Throughout the week I was my mother's daughter – staying silent, not sure what to do with all the thoughts in my head. I took the easy route and followed the same routine with Wayne: dinner at six, kitchen cleanup, goodnight baths, and then books for the boys.

54

Chapter 11

In Too Deep

Gracious, what a sight he was! Back from a three-week vacation, Robert waltzed in radiating a sun-kissed smile to all. Before long, when I stood alone in the hall, Dr. R eased up alongside me. "Come to my office." His voice calm but deadly serious.

The ring of phones, the click of the copy machine, the hum of patient chatter drifted away to muffled sounds as we entered his office.

Straightway, he asked it: "Did you go to counseling?"

Instantly my face grew hot. "Yes. First with both of us, and then in separate sessions. I've gone several more times, and Wayne has gone once more."

"How do you feel about that?" he asked.

My heart skipped. I liked it that he wanted to know how I was doing. "I think the counselor senses my frustrations with Wayne and the kids."

Then from out of nowhere, I heard myself say, "I'm going to confront the counselor about asking Wayne for a break in our relationship." Even the calmness of my voice shocked me as my heart hammered in my chest. But the words were out. I needed to know: Were we friends or more? Or not? Waiting,

55

I stood with an earthquake pounding in my chest.

"A break would be good for you." He said the words matter-of-factly, in his own smooth way.

In that one sentence, that one smile, Robert eased all my misgivings. My heart lightened as I soaked up the moment. Shamefully, I heard what I wanted to hear.

Before I could blink, Robert added, "I'll be right back." He stepped into the reception area and chatted with Peggy, the office employee who scheduled appointments. A moment later he returned to my side. He gently leaned in toward my ear, and the words quietly emerged. "I scheduled an hour for lunch. I want to take you to my condo to show you something."

Any sensible brain cells I had working inside my head screamed *No!* But my drumming heart pushed to seek out what he wanted me to see.

I made my way to the passenger side of his elite Cadillac Eldorado Biarritz convertible. Opening the door, I got a whiff of leather and elegance so unlike my practical compact Chevette. I slid into the plush bucket seat that nestled up to Robert's. As we headed south of town, he said, "I've moved in and feel pretty settled."

He pulled into a sprawling complex of new one-level condos wedged among the towering leafless March oak trees.

A lone birch stood among them. A part of me felt as out of place as that birch because I was a married lady. Yet, like the fallen scattered leaves, any moral goodness I once embraced was being whisked away by Robert's charms.

We got out of the car, stepped through the condo doorway, and a whiff of fresh paint filled the air. He led me past the living room that was graced with a baby grand piano, down the hall and then swung open a set of doublewide doors. "This is a storage closet, but it's big. I thought it would even be big enough for you to use as an art studio."

Art studio? I gasped.

Robert was planning a studio for me! I let my thoughts drift, imagining my watercolor brush spreading paint in mystical colors. As the calm and quiet of the condo embraced me, I mentally sketched myself here, enjoying art with him.

He cradled my cheek in the palm of his hand. I reached up and curved my hand around the back of his neck. I felt his pulse thump. It beat crazy-fast like mine. As he locked his arms around my waist, he kissed me. No one had ever kissed me the way he did. Intense, but not hard. Sweet, but not soft. He held my heart entirely in his hands.

When he drew away, he said, "I'm taking a Spanish class. It's something I've never done before, and I love it. The learning, the challenge. You need to become your own person. Not just what others want or expect. Understand?"

I nodded. It was enough for me to throw caution aside as I pictured the new life he painted for me so clearly. Robert was trying new things. I wanted to latch on and be right there exploring new things, too.

"You were meant for larger things. Much larger things and I can give you those."

As soon as the words were out of his mouth, my insides hummed telling me how hungry I had been since the Christmas party for him to say he wanted me. Now in March, he finally clarified his back and forth thoughts of our relationship. I clung to the thought that Robert could solve all the struggles I had at the oh, so predictable Colonial, never questioning why he appeared suddenly confident about us.

"I know this trip to the condo feels rushed, but I wanted to share this with you." He gave me that glowing smile. "We need to get back to the office."

Riding back, my head swirled with questions. I managed one. "What's next?"

"Where are you with Wayne?"

An uncomfortable wave washed over my body. Wayne. The boys. My cheeks burned with heat and the back of my neck tightened.

What I felt for Robert was indescribably powerful, especially after what we'd just shared in his condo. He turned his gaze to me and I held it for a few seconds. Those eyes drew me in. Without thinking, I blurted out. "We have a counseling session tonight. I'm going to ask for a place of my own." My own mouth gaped open at my reckless words. *Where did this come from?*

Robert broke into that radiant smile.

"I think that's a good idea." His smile widened.

I melted in my seat. It happened any time, every time, when he smiled at me like that. In that moment, I foolishly let myself be swept away. I convinced myself that the happiness Robert gave me was good for me.

Back at the office, I somehow composed myself and pushed aside the undertow of emotion that raced through my head. I got through my shift and headed home.

Chapter 12
Walking Away

That day in late-March became the longest day of my life as I selfishly made the hardest decision in my life. Alone at counseling, I let out all my shut-in emotions and poured out my intent to leave Wayne.

"Is that what you feel is best?" the counselor asked.

"I want to try." I hung my head. "The only way for me to separate is to walk away from the Colonial ... from everything."

"Everything?"

"Wayne will never give up the boys so it will have to be me who leaves."

"How do you feel about that?"

"Awful." I clutched the armrest of my chair for support. "I am causing so much disruption."

The counselor hit me with more painful questions: What kind of visitation would I suggest? Would Wayne go along with it?

The ugly and raw reality of what I was about to do grabbed me around the neck and began to squeeze. I didn't enjoy causing other people hurt. I knew there was no such thing as gradually breaking someone's heart. There was always going to be The Moment, the instant when the knife pierces the heart. When all the plans and hopes in a relationship die. When the real ugliness begins.

Returning home after counseling, I argued with myself for a long while, wrestling with the severity of the turmoil I was about to cause.

Suddenly Wayne was home. He walked past me and I felt it, the stifling tension in the air between us. I coached myself on: *You've got to do it, face it, take the ache and use it to get you where you need to go.*

Breaking the silence, I pulled out a chair at the kitchen table and asked, "Can we sit down?"

Heaviness hung between us. The only sound was the furnace clicking on as the boys slept above us. Wayne settled into a chair opposite me.

I mustered every ounce of directness I could find. "I can't do this anymore. Us, that is."

Wayne detected the change in my voice.

This was The Moment.

He was breathing and blinking fast, and I could see a nervous gulp in his throat. He dropped his gaze to the table and immediately organized the boys' mess of crayons into a neat row. "Why?"

"It's not you, it's me. I feel trapped."

"How can I help?" He straightened the already straight crayons.

"Let me go."

"Go where?" I heard the desperation in his voice that had always been so laid-back.

"A place of my own."

"You mean away from here?" His voice tensed, almost in terror.

Time seemed to stop. I felt the tremor as Wayne's life foundation crumbled. He lifted his eyes to meet mine, and now anger bored at me. "You'll never take the boys from me."

A hot wetness filled my eyes and I tried to blink it away. I knew Wayne would never leave the Colonial or the boys, but hearing the words slapped me back to reality.

A sense of dread filled me as I thought of having to separate from the boys.

"So you're walking away, Kathy?" Wayne challenged me.

I nodded. I avoided my feelings for Robert, convincing myself that by doing so I was helping Wayne. But that was a moral charade.

He slammed the table with a fist and stormed out of the room.

An agonizing maternal instinct tugged at my conscience. *How could I separate myself from the boys?* A mother was supposed to protect her young. Was I doing the right thing? A custody battle with Wayne would put our sons in the middle of a war zone. Already they had suffered through my unhappiness. I couldn't let them be harmed further. I had to be the one to suffer the harshness of Wayne's determination for custody of the boys.

I heard water running through the pipes. Wayne had gone upstairs and was in the shower. I gathered a pillow and blanket and shuffled to the living room. I curled directly onto the floor. It was the first time I wouldn't be crawling out of the upstairs bed after endless hours of tossing. As I cowered, the wind whistled from outside. A chill ran through me and sent a hollowness that made my insides feel like that wind was rushing through me.

Sleep wouldn't come. I thrashed about trying to come

up with a way that I could see the boys on a weekly basis without disrupting their lives. I knew I had to find a full-time job to support myself, and I would probably need to contribute child support if Wayne became the major parent. These thoughts tore through my heart, but I had to face them.

On top of those thoughts, guilt grew and gnawed at me. I was too weak to admit my adulterous ways to Wayne ... or anyone. I told myself I would simply try out a place of my own to test the waters and see how I could manage outside the cocoon that was the Colonial. Robert had his place and I would have mine. There was time to see what would happen. Finally, I fell into a hazy sleep.

In the morning I heard Wayne come downstairs. I stayed hidden in a huddle until I heard the click as he shut the kitchen door and left for work.

The boys awoke, and as I served cereal in a daze, the phone rang. Robert's tenor voice eased a soothing "Hello." My mouth dropped open. He had never called me at home!

"How was your session last night?"

"Uh." My throat went dry and my heart sped up a notch.

"Take a breath," he coached me, his voice switching to low and serious.

I let out the breath I didn't realize I was holding. He knew me so well.

"Now tell me about last night."

Three seconds into the phone call, Robert's soothing voice provided all the emotional fuel I needed to fill me with calmness and certainty as I told him about the evening.

In the days ahead, Wayne and I struggled. His jaw locked tight each time we talked, and I sensed he was coping by going numb to everything.

The days crawled along as we broached the subject of an apartment for me, crossed into visitation, which dredged up child support. I knew a nursing job in a hospital setting could support me, but not with child support in the mix. With Wayne staying in the Colonial, I offered to give him my equity in the house instead of child support. Wayne knew this meant thousands of dollars over time, so he agreed. The choice seemed fair to me; I felt the boys deserved the security the Colonial gave them.

Such discussions with Wayne were exhausting with emotions running high for both of us. The turbulence didn't end there. When alone with the boys, I felt a jumble of emotions – shame, fear, guilt – tugging me in different directions, questioning my actions. Often I fell into a stupor while attempting to sift through the chaos that filled my head. I was in a hurtful state of confusion, at times full of despair. Then, when I would be at my lowest, Robert would call and lull me into a calmer place where the *Tonka* would ease.

As I pressed forward, the next step was to face my mother.

Chapter 13

Goodbye is a Painful Word

I had coiled the telephone cord so tightly around my index finger that it turned white, yet I hadn't noticed. All of my concentration focused on the *ring!* echoing in my ear, awaiting Mom's voice on the other end.

When she said hello, my chest heaved. Somehow I squeaked out my news.

"You're giving up on your marriage?"

The blow was swift and blasted a hole through my chest. I sat there frozen, paralyzed by her words.

"I stuck it out for almost forty years with your father. If I can do it, you can do it." Her voice pulsed through the receiver. "Did you get the apron pattern I sent you? It's simple to sew."

"I tried all the crafts. They just ..."

"I know, you told me before, but I don't understand," she said. "We sent you to that art camp, but you choose to be a nurse. What are you looking for?"

Guilt surrounded me. My parents had given me so much. As my heart slid up to my throat, I felt myself backpedal. "Ah,

I've been enjoying the challenge of watercolor."

"Well, it's good you're painting for your hobby."

My palm turned sweaty clutching the phone receiver. I was avoiding the reason I called. "The counselor thought a separation from Wayne ..."

"Counselor? Who would support something like this? In my day there was never a thing called divorce."

I felt myself withdrawing, as I knew I was crushing her.

"Kathleen, if you do this you're pulling the rug out from under all of us, not just the boys," Mom said. "How can you do that? You need to act like an adult."

The pause on the other end of the line seemed endless. I knew mom was trying to be supportive, but at that time in my life, I couldn't grasp how to apply her wisdom so it would help me.

The subsequent click, although barely audible, was as if Mom had just screamed in my ear.

Her distressing words were too difficult to hold onto so I stuffed them down deep. Overwhelmed, I let in the soft whispering words that did comfort me. Robert's: "When do you move into your apartment? How is your job search coming?"

I interviewed at the local hospital where I had worked years earlier. As expected, they had an opening on the brutal night shift. It was an ugly eight-hour shift, which meant trying to sleep during the day so I could stay up all night. At times it seemed like the punishment I deserved for "giving up" on my marriage, as my mother reminded me. In reality, the harsh shift would be a picnic compared to the awful task of telling the boys I was leaving.

One Sunday in April, I gathered every ounce of courage and squatted down next to my sons as they stood side by side facing me. Wayne stood behind me. The counselor had coached me on key words, yet it didn't make what I had to do any easier. I wasn't just nervous; I was terrified. I set my jaw and did my best.

"I have something important to tell you." My chest felt too tight for my lungs; I tried to steady my voice. "Your dad and I won't be living together any more. You'll still live here with dad, go to the same school, and play with the same friends." My lungs were burning for air, yet I knew it was really my heart breaking down the middle. I pushed ahead, afraid if I stopped, I'd collapse. "I have a different house that you'll visit next Saturday. Then I'll see you every Tuesday and alternating weekends." I reached up and tugged Wayne's arm, pulling him down to our level. "We will always be your mom and dad." I kept my hand clutched to Wayne's arm; otherwise, I was afraid the boys would see it shaking. "We love you and this is not your fault."

As I looked into my boys' eyes there was trust and love, and I even saw a calmness cross their faces. Kids know more than you think. I snatched them into a bear hug. Adam squeezed back, but Brian's stance stayed rigid. "Is there a playground at our new house?" Adam asked.

"Yes, there's a two-story jungle gym."

That's all it took for Brian to melt into my arms, too, and a smile split his lips.

At the small apartment I rented, I buried myself in unpacking my personal belongings and arranged my childhood bedroom set from the guest room in the Colonial. Old wicker furniture became the living room decor. As much as I tried these new-apartment chores didn't distract me from getting the jitters as I thought about the boys' impending first visit.

I was entering foreign territory here. Wayne had the advantage of the same beds as usual, the same school routine. His fondness for routine gave me comfort knowing that part of the boys' life would be consistent. As I waited for their initial visit, my stomach felt like it was riding on a roller coaster. I had no idea what was coming: Would the visit be a slow emotional rise uphill or an immediate plunge of panic?

On Friday I waited in the apartment parking lot, trying to find comfort from the balmy seventy-degree April day for this first exchange. Right on time, Wayne pulled in. As he parked, the boys spotted me, unbuckled their seat belts, and bolted from the car. They embraced me at the waist and I kissed their chest-high heads. Through teary eyes, I gazed down at their big grins that cracked across their faces, and felt their unconditional love.

"Playground!" they shouted as they spied the fortress that was not more than a Frisbee toss away. "Can we go?"

I blinked away the watery eyes. "Sure, just don't wander off. I'll be there in a minute."

The boys scurried off, and Wayne handed over their backpacks. He looked right at me and we had an awkward moment. It was that vacant space where there were a thousand things to say and yet ... nothing to say. In the earlier weeks, in counseling and at home, we had said so much and so little.

I cleared my throat. "Sunday at six?"

"Don't be late," he said, turning away. I saw his gaze shift over to the boys. They were bouncing from slides to swings. He walked over and gave them each a big squeeze, sharing words of reassurance, I was certain. Wayne always put the boys first.

As I drifted over to a playground bench, Wayne headed to his car without a glance my way.

The boys frolicked about. My sons were as connected as peanut butter and jelly, yet different. Adam, the younger of the two, walked right up to a kid about his height that was playing nearby. Without hesitation, Adam asked, "Do you want to be my friend?" Brian, the more cautions of the two, hung a step back, not uttering a word. It was just part of his quiet nature.

The new kid smiled. "Sure, I'll be your friend. Where do you live?"

"Here." Adam waved his arm in no particular direction toward the multi-dwelling complex of three story buildings where I now lived.

That was the clue to raise Brian's interest. He hustled over to me to get more information. I pointed to the nearby sliding glass doors of our ground-level apartment. After gaining the knowledge from me that he needed, Brian seemed much more at ease. In fact, he hurried back to join a growing number of kids swarming the playground.

The knot in my stomach eased a bit as the boys slid into the group. This boatload-of-kids playground was much better than our two-seated swing set in the lonely backyard of the Colonial.

Throughout the weekend the boys invited me to join their playground fortress. "Come on, Mom. Let's build a train."

Wedged between them, I teetered on the top of a sky-scraper-high slide and feared for my life.

"Just hang onto to me!" Brian yelled, then snagged my arms and pulled them around his waist.

"You're in for the best ride of your life!" Adam yelled.

With that, we were off! The wind soared and my hair flew

in every direction. At the bottom we landed in a heap and giggled with glee.

"Hurry! Let's go again!" Brian squealed.

The exhilaration I felt wasn't from the screaming speed of the ride, but from the joy we were experiencing together. It had been a long, long time since we tumbled together with such ease.

On Sunday we headed back to the Colonial. I felt sudden tension, realizing this was the death drop of that roller coaster: Saying goodbye.

However, like the earlier drop-off, the boys darted from the Chevette, this time into Wayne's arms. Then they launched onto their beloved two-wheeler bikes, pulling wheelies and braking into slides. I barely got a wave of farewell from the boys. Although the ease in which the boys flowed from the exchange comforted me, it didn't ease the sadness that filled my heart from having to say goodbye. Even the perky spring daffodils bobbing in the breeze didn't brighten my mood.

Two things did help ease the emptiness: The art and the doctor.

Painting provided me with a serenity and challenge that I hadn't found in any other craft. Ten minutes into the fluidity of watercolor, something unexpected happened. A feeling of delight surged through me as I tried to solve the mysterious movement of paint across the wet paper. I had been fortunate that, every month or so, I had sold a small painting at the Robin Gallery. I had even gotten a positive critique from the art editor of the local newspaper after he visited the gallery.

Swinging the paintbrush one day, I dabbed the wings of a blue bird. The faded edges of the image pleasingly simulated flight.

Adding to the synergy I felt from painting was having Robert in my life. His romantic ways lifted my tired body, mind, and heart. Weekly I received gifts: a health club membership, work-out clothes (including legwarmers from the video aerobics icon of the era, Jane Fonda), and my favorite ... a sleek, off-the-shoulder teal cocktail dress along with a weekend getaway to wear it!

As we melted into summer, I was smitten by this man and our new rhythm. There was time for us, time for me to be with the boys, time for Robert to be with his kids, and time for his Wednesday night Spanish lesson. I respected his privacy, never doubting his actions, and attacked my new life with a paintbrush in hand.

Chapter 14
Hurtful Thoughts

I inhaled that perfect Lake Michigan air – cool and unspoiled and just a little mossy. We had been cruising in the Cadillac for about twenty minutes when Robert eased the car up to a lake front restaurant nestled along the shoreline. It was picturesque, with the summer waves frothing nearby. Driving out of town was typical for us when we went dining or getting lost among the museums or music concerts of larger cities. Despite the privacy of these trips, a buzz began regarding our scandal.

The moment I pulled up to the Colonial to drop off the boys, I saw the hard line that tugged tight across Wayne's lips and knew he had heard an earful.

Sure enough, as soon as the boy scooted off to shoot basketballs, Wayne snarled, "So ... the doctor?"

I had no choice but to spill it and all its ugliness. "We've been dating."

"It's more than that, from what a neighbor told me. She said she saw his car parked once in this driveway during the middle of the day! Was it going on when you lived *here*?" His eyes seared and his voice trembled. A vein in his left temple bulged and pulsed.

"What? No! Hold on..." I stammered as I tried to remember when Robert had been over. Then it dawned on me. He had stopped by after Brian had stitches. At the time, it had been such a quick visit, I never thought much about it. Before I could explain, Wayne interrupted me.

"How long has this been going on behind my back?" Wayne jumped to a conclusion before I could explain. "How could you?" This time his voice softened and his stance shrunk. Instantly, he looked small. Blank. Broken.

"I'm sorry. We started out as friends ..." my voice trailed off as I tried to find the words.

Wayne suddenly straightened his shoulders, and his eyes fired at me as he waited for more.

"It just sort of happened," I said.

His stare became so intense it caught my breath. I had to look away.

"You cheated on me, Kathy! I don't even know who you are anymore," he yelled, throwing his hands in the air.

I didn't respond. *What could I say?*

Wayne took the lead. "You said you needed time away from us. Well, guess what. We need time away from you. I cannot be a part of your disloyalty." He spread out his words, avoiding contractions. "You will get papers in the mail from my attorney." He spun on his heel and stalked off to the boys.

I let him go. In actuality I had probably let him go months before when Robert's support whisked me away. Once I moved from the Colonial, Wayne and I had continued separate counseling sessions, and I never asked to meet with Wayne again. If I were honest with myself, I was too wrapped up in Robert. He seemed to have the answers I wanted to hear.

When news of my new romance with Robert surfaced,

most of our mutual friends migrated to Wayne's side. Statistics supported his underdog status. Back in the mid-eighties, he was in the minority. Only 9 percent of the primary caregivers in our situation were the dads, compared with 72 percent of the moms having primary custody. Wayne was the hero, and I was the villain. It was as if I had a scarlet letter "A" on my chest.

One Tuesday evening, as I dropped off the boys at the Colonial, Gloria, my neighbor to the west, was out hauling a lawn sprinkler. A typical sight. Gloria's two boys were in high school, and she spent her days staying home and being loyal to things like a rigid watering regimen.

She took a few steps closer to me and gave me a scowl as if I were a grub that ate away at her lawn. "Since you've been gone, Wayne's given up on trying to keep one eye on the boys and one eye on the lawn." She narrowed her eyes at me and then at Wayne's lawn: crisp and brown and weedy. The opposite of her brilliant-green, pristine turf.

"It's a lot to juggle," I said.

"More than a lot. The poor man. I look at him and my heart breaks. I don't know how you could have walked away from those two precious angels. All so you could flit around. Someone should have knocked some sense into you, but no ..."

At this point she turned her back on me. Completely deflated, I slithered away. I couldn't get back to Robert's embrace fast enough. He gave me the positive attention I needed, and I soaked it all up.

Between Robert and my watercolor studies, I found comfort. I would dip my brush into the opaqueness of a Cerulean blue and mix it with the transparent sparkle of Brown Madder. Onto wet paper, I brushed the bluish-green mixture and watched in awe as the two paints separated in some places but held as one in others. This was the mystery of this medium, and every time I tried to conquer the paints, or at least understand them, a thrill rushed through me.

At my apartment one morning, a knock on the sliding glass doors made me look up. Robert. The rising sun of the pleasant day beamed a soothing backdrop behind the man at the door. He flashed his magical smile and my heart soared.

Entering through the sliders, he stepped over to my painting in progress, pouring over the burst of pink fuchsia blooms framed in green foliage.

"It's for the art fair," I said. Months earlier I had been juried by a panel of judges and accepted into my first summer show, now just a few weeks off.

"You'll do great." Robert hovered close as he examined my work.

I wished I had his confidence. I had sold a few pieces at the gallery, but it was never during my shift as artist on duty. This time I would be right out there with my art, exposed and vulnerable to every comment. *What if they snickered at my simple work?*

While I paused from my work, paintbrush in hand, Robert laced his fingers through my free hand. The touch brought me back to the moment ... which was a big one.

"Bring the boys right over to my place and we'll leave for the farm," he said. "I'm ready to go."

This was the first time I was going to meet Robert's family, and his first outing with the boys. I felt my palms turn sweaty, and the paintbrush dropped right out of my hand.

He bent to pick up the brush. "Just bring the boys and leave your worries at home."

My chest swelled. He was supportive of my art, my kids, and me!

In less than forty minutes, we rolled into the hilly terrain of the Michigan countryside where grain silos were the tallest structures around. Robert steered the Cadillac onto a two-track and gave us a guided tour. "Cranky Clarence's orchard is on the right," he said, waving toward cherry trees brimming with fruit. "My brother Tim's beans are on the left." There were mile-long rows of leafy soybeans.

"Is Clarence part of your family, too?" Adam asked.

Robert shot my son a sly smile in the rearview mirror and gave a mellow chuckle. "No, you won't be meeting Cranky Clarence. But you're going to love all the kids here. See there?" Robert said while pointing through the windshield. "The hayride is starting. Let's hustle!"

Five minutes later the boys were atop a mound of straw, bouncing along with more than twenty kids as a towing tractor rumbled and puffed its clouds of diesel exhaust. Adam chatted with a boy his age that had a Band-Aid on each knee and mud on his cheeks. They could have passed for twins. Brian was fine, too. He beamed a smile my way so big it almost squeezed his eyes shut. It warmed my heart.

That left me to face Robert's mom. She stood drill-sergeant stiff, her silver curls wound tight. "Welcome." She reached out her hand, and I offered mine. She clamped on with a death grip and tugged my hand up and down a few times.

I tried to smile.

"Glad you could come" were the words, but her lips drew tight and her smile forced.

"Thank you." My voice was shaky and I sensed some murmurs nearby. Various relatives stared at us and whispered.

Enter Robert's winning personality. He flashed his baby blues and soon had the group engaged with his smooth groove of informative chitchat. Finding comfort at Robert's side, I didn't stray too far.

In a short while, the hayride returned, the tractor thumping its way up the rutted road, stopping to let off the riders.

"Who's going to be *'it'* for Kick the Can?" asked a teen boy whose hair stuck out like a tuft of straw on a scarecrow.

Everyone seemed to be up for Kick the Can, a game of hide 'n seek tag, including a fireplug of a kid who stepped out from behind the teenager. "I'll be 'it.'"

A tin coffee can was set upside down in the farmyard, and the game was on!

"One, two, three ..." the short one counted, eyes closed, as kids scurried to hide.

Everyone played and played until late afternoon, when it was time to head home. Burrowed in the back of the Cadillac, the boys jabbered about the hayride, the kids, the games. I felt a thrill in my chest hearing my sons' merriment. Robert gave me a wink, and my heart expanded in my chest.

Then, from out the car window as we drove off, I caught a glimpse of Robert's mom. Her smile looked pasted on. It reminded of my own mother.

Chapter 15
Ardent Art Fair

Daybreak rose hot and humid on the mid-August morning of my first art fair. As I loaded my work into the Chevette, I became drenched in sweat. A swarm of tiny sand flies discovered me and hovered around my head. Mosquitoes gorged on my bare legs. With my arms crammed with art, I tried to shoo away the little flies with a swish of my shoulder-length hair. No luck. They showed no mercy. As it turned out, the hot and buggy start was the easiest part of my day.

With the subcompact jam-packed, I chugged along to the neighboring town thirty miles away, roasting all the way. Even with the windows cranked down, the non-air-conditioned car was a pizza oven. My thoughts, meanwhile, simmered with insecurity. This was my first public display where I would be within earshot of every comment. *Could I take the heat?*

Fortunately, I had little time to fret. Upon arriving, I circled around the grassy park looking for the art fair spot No. 89. I discovered my assigned destination was at the entrance, on a patch of cement. I didn't expect this. Weeks earlier, a fellow Robin Gallery artist had shared some valuable art fair pointers, including how to set up on a grassy patch. Here,

My 1982 Chevette packed for an art fair

now, on the cement, the tent stakes he graciously lent me for securing my tall display were useless. His words haunted me as I stared at the concrete pad: "If you don't anchor the lightweight frame, one gust of wind, and the display will spin in mid-air like Dorothy's house in Kansas."

I was in the midst of an army of artists scurrying to set out their wares.

In a daze, I lugged the first load to my designated space. Next to me, a burly man hefted cinder blocks to anchor his display onto the cement.

"Howdy! Name's Hank," he said with a neighborly wave and then wiped his sweaty brow.

As if on cue, a gust of hot wind whipped me in the face

and reminded me of the mess I faced. I had to do something. "It's my first show. And I brought tent stakes!"

He blew out a long, low whistle. Then he sang sweet words. "Just unload and I'll hitch you up to my booth. And take these." He handed me a wad of huge rubber bands. "Stretch them around each painting so the art won't sail away in the wind."

There was so much to learn and endure. I began setting up my tall racks when, from behind, I heard, "Juried entry form and sales tax permit, please." It was the fair director armed with a clipboard an inch thick with papers.

Certain both were in my makeshift office – Tupperware container of pens, receipt book, and calculator in case I actually made a sale – I rifled through the box and pulled out the tax permit. "I must have left the entry form at home."

"No form. No show," she announced.

My heart pounded as I remembered the hours it took to fill out the lengthy entry form and photograph my artwork to land a coveted spot in this juried show. I slapped on the bravest smile and said, "I have a copy of the congratulatory letter I received from you."

As her eyes scanned the letter, she said, "I'll make an exception this time."

By this time my skin had swelled from the bug bites earlier. The sand fly pinpricks had swollen to the size of match heads while the mosquito bite mounds were mountains in between. I scratched at my arm, uncertain if my itchy-twitchy state was from the bug bites. More than likely the itchiness was from nerves. *Would someone here actually peel off some cash and slap it into my palm for something I created?*

The day progressed and I baked in the sweltering air, yet the wonderful people I met made it all worthwhile. They came from miles around. I gobbled up every ooh and ah. My skin prickled, and not from the heat or bug bites but from the smiles my art elicited.

Then ... I sold a painting!

A decent size one, too!

As I took it off the rack, I beamed at the work with pride. Geraniums gushed out of a basket. I had labored on every bloom, with layers of the lucent burgundy color, Alizarin Crimson, determined that some buds had crisp edges while others faded away. It thrilled me to think that someone admired my efforts!

Later, when I patted the cash in my pocket, pride rushed through me even though the hundred dollars from selling just one piece wouldn't come close to what I had invested in supplies. Instead, I thought, not bad for a rookie!

At dusk I packed up and motored home. Earlier in the week, Robert had invited me to dinner after the fair. When my Chevette pulled up on the pad behind his condo garage, he stepped outside, opened my car door, and handed me a congratulatory glass of white wine. I took a sip, letting the chilled liquid ease the heat of the long day.

He reached for a nearby green leafy bush, plucked a snow-ball size bloom, and passed it to me by the stem. "You look like you could use this. It's a hydrangea. Smell it."

I slowly breathed in the sweet perfume-like scent, letting the fragrance fill me.

He shut the car door behind me, backed me against it, reached his palm to caress the nape of my neck and said softly, "Rough day?"

As he nuzzled his face into mine, I realized it had been rough. And perfect.

Chapter 16

A Taste of North Dakota

Among the people I once called friends, an undercurrent of ugliness circled. In addition to considering me a bad mother who had dropped a bomb on her family, everyone had an opinion about what I ought to do next. "You should be 'fighting' for your kids ... You should just up and 'yank' them from their dad."

All that unsolicited advice preyed on me. This growing current of ugliness caused my heart to take notice when Robert asked one day, "What would you think of relocating? Getting a fresh start. Starting over someplace new?"

"What do you mean?"

"I had a recruiter call me. It's from a place I never considered moving, but after listening to the amenities and reviewing this material, I think we should at least take the interview." He slid a packet across the table.

I followed the legal-size envelope with my eyes as it moved over to me. *We. He said we, as in him and me.* We would be together away from the brutal words that bit to my core. The

81

world fell away, drained except for my homey thoughts of the two of us.

"It's to Bismarck, North Dakota."

"How far away is that?"

"You'll be able to fly back to see the boys whenever you want, and you can have them come out during school breaks," he said, quickly addressing the biggest hurdle for me to even consider taking such a leap. He reached across the table and nestled his hand in mine.

"You could look for a job that is art related instead of another night shift of nursing."

This man really was after my heart.

"At least we should visit and see what the place is all about."

My emotions were raw from all the months of every-body meddling in my life, so when his eyes searched mine, I inhaled his steady strength. "I guess we could at least look."

Before the big trip, Robert sent me shopping for new dresses from street-smart to shimmering. After that, all I had to do was show up on his doorstep at the appointed time with my suitcase packed. The recruiters had planned the entire weekend for us, beginning with a stretch Lincoln Town Car that eased up to the curb. The comfort didn't end there.

Soon we relaxed in the airline luxury of first class seats, sipping champagne. Somewhere over Minnesota, Robert took out a small box and placed the warm fur of velvet in my palm.

"Open it," he nudged me.

I flipped open the plush lid. A radiant ring boasting a blue gemstone sparkled on a satin pillow, almost blinding me.

"It's aquamarine." He slipped it out of the box.

The luscious color matched his magical blue eyes. I felt as if I were floating on the clouds below our plane.

While holding the ring in one hand, he caressed my left hand with his other. "I think we should pose as married for the executives who will be interviewing us. You know ... first impressions and all. I brought a ring for me to start wearing, too." He pulled a gold band from his coat pocket and slid it on his left ring finger. Then he extended the aquamarine. "The ring is yours to keep. Consider it a promise for more."

Perhaps the radiant ring mesmerized me or perhaps the bubbly brew, but my thumping heart convinced me I didn't need a marriage certificate to prove our commitment to each other. I felt that this ring signified Robert's promise that we were a steady, long-term couple. I never thought I needed clarification. I uttered yes and let the ring dance on my finger. Robert's offer was my own private ceremony! Already I felt free from the Michigan agony in this new place where I left my baggage behind.

Bismarck could charm like Robert. Upon arrival, I noticed the wide-open prairie stretched as far as the eye could see. At the edge of town, the Missouri River flowed so wide a dinner-cruise paddleboat became a speck on the water. The riverbank glowed with the brilliant golds of cottonwood leaves that swished in the autumn air. It was a different sound than the foghorns and surf of Lake Michigan, yet just as beautiful.

Downtown held a mix of classic buildings, updated in a noble fashion. The medical facility was state-of-the-art, and the people, well ... they were real.

"Hello! Welcome!" The men I encountered gripped my hand in a double-clad grasp and pumped it like an oil rig. When they finally released it, they latched onto my shoulder and gave me a hearty sway. As for the ladies, they sang out "hello" and swept me into hugs that squeezed until I wriggled free.

All weekend we were invited into their homes for meals and parties, mingling with locals of German and Scandinavian heritage as well as transplants like us. Autumn delicacies, from schnitzel to brisket to dumplings, graced the tables.

"Try one of my handmade venison Bratwurst. My brother took the buck down himself," said a round man with thinning gray hair. He was offering a tray full of small plumped sausages. His hands were look-alike meaty and chubby. "Geese and pheasant are my favorite, but I drool for the deer brats, too. It's a secret recipe."

A spicy tang wafted from his tray. I snagged a pudgy link and bit through the delicately thin casing. "Mmm." The punch of cardamom tickled my tongue.

The weekend flew by. In every home, at every meeting, we were treated like friends since childhood. Their words rang with honesty and sincerity.

On the plane ride home, we sat stunned. Neither of us had anticipated such a warm reception and a stellar work environment. Added to the mix of emotion was the comfort of not being judged, like back at home.

Finally, Robert spoke. "It's a big decision. Let's get through the holidays before we take this any further." Then he hit a button on the armrest and my seat tilted back to match his. He twined his fingers through mine and closed his eyes. I saw the rise and fall of his chest; when I drifted off, we were breathing in unison.

The peaceful sleep was short-lived, though. I woke with my heart knocking in my chest as a nap-induced vision of the boys flashed through my mind. All weekend I had pushed away the thoughts of how far this location was from them. As I quietly struggled to catch my breath, it was obvious I didn't have my fears under control. My eyes stung with tears and my chest tightened as I tried to settle. Then I felt Robert squeeze my hand while his eyes remained closed. "You don't have to make a decision for a while. We can take our time."

My heart rate calmed as I let Robert's words comfort me. I shoved the strained feelings down deep. Getting through the holidays would be difficult enough.

* * *

Knowing Wayne didn't like change, I was a bit edgy when I confronted him, "Next week, can I see the boys on Wednesday instead of Tuesday?"

"What's the problem?" he asked.

"I have a schedule conflict."

"Like what?" I heard a bite to his words.

I couldn't blame him for being angry so I took the easy way and avoided his remark. "I just have a schedule conflict, but I would still like to see the boys."

"Yeah, you'd like to see the boys when it's convenient for you. Why do you need to change? Is it work?" He folded his arms across his chest, waiting for an answer.

"No, it's not work, but I'd like to attend an event and I have a ticket." I stopped there. I had a date with Robert, yet I didn't want to wave that in his face.

"An event? That's more important than your sons? You're thoughtless. I can't even depend on you for one night." His nostrils flared and his jaw set tight. "I don't understand you anymore. Unless you have an emergency I am not resched-uling."

"That's fine. I'll be here next Tuesday." I turned and walked away, unsurprised by Wayne's rigidity. His anger, no doubt, was also to remind me how this whole thing was my fault. However, the pull to Robert was stronger than any desire I had to "work" on my marriage with Wayne. I convinced myself I had "worked" with Wayne for more than a decade. Whereas, my efforts with Robert felt like no "work" at all.

Shortly, after the confrontation about the schedule change with Wayne, the divorce papers arrived in the mail. The words on the paper became blurry. I broke out in a cold sweat as tightness in my chest spread all over my body. Signing this was so final. There were moments, dozens of them every single day, when guilt overcame me. However, for some serious reasons I couldn't go back to the Colonial on Lancelot Road. To many people, the Colonial subdivision was a remarkable place. To me, the newly constructed homes, paved roads, and streets named after Camelot were far from utopia.

I signed the papers.

Chapter 17

Better Than Santa Claus

Hundreds of tiny white Christmas lights blinked rapidly. For the upcoming holiday Robert had decorated his condo using fresh pine boughs and garland, and I couldn't get enough of that sensational evergreen scent. Engrossed in the holiday spirit, he played for me Tchaikovsky's *Nutcracker* on his baby grand piano. I soaked up every note, closing my eyes and drifting into the magic of it all.

Suddenly the music stopped. Robert glanced up from the keyboard, his eyes dancing in some creative reverie. "I think you should create a Christmas card!" he declared.

"A Christmas card?" I repeated, trying to catch up with whatever his thoughts were concocting.

"Sure, sure. With a distinctive verse!" He rose from the piano bench, dashed to the study, and came back waving a hardcover book of famous quotes. It was such a thick old book he could hardly grip the spine with one hand.

He flipped through the pages, stopped midway, and traced some small print with his finger. "Dylan Thomas is one of my favorite authors. Listen to this. It's perfect for a

Christmas card." His voice took on a soft cadence.

"I sometimes hear a moment before sleep that I can never remember, whether it snowed for six days and six nights when I was twelve, or whether it snowed for twelve days and twelve nights when I was six."

That's all it took for me to picture a cottage bundled under a blanket of snow. In addition, I would use a blue-tint watercolor for the sky, and a dry brush for the texture of the rough, woody cabin. "I'd love to paint a winter scene," I said.

"Painting is good, but we need to mail at least twenty of our cards."

I blinked in confusion. "You want to mail my artwork?"

"Sure. If you draw the winter scene in black ink like you did designing the medical office pamphlet, then we can use the same print shop."

I had forgotten about the cover design he asked me to create. The office gave away thousands of those printed brochures. At the time, I felt honored that he asked me to do that job. To think Robert wanted me to design "our" Christmas card made my heart sing its own merry tune.

However, with the holidays on my mind, memories hit me more intensely than the hundred-times-a-day thoughts I already had about the boys. The gripping chokehold of *Tonka* had shifted to an ache of simply missing them.

With determination, I tamped it down and looked about, now studying my apartment. Eight months earlier when I left the Colonial behind, I had also left all the holiday ornaments and trimmings behind. Christmas was an important tradition, and Wayne thrived on familiar customs and routines. If decorations made Wayne's life easier, I reasoned, then the boys' life would be easier.

As I scanned the apartment, a few ideas came to my mind. I hauled out my sewing machine to create stockings for the boys, a tradition they were familiar with and one I could easily sustain.

Next I trimmed paper strips for us to loop and string together to create paper-chain garland. I felt my heart lighten as I doubled the quantity of paper, knowing the boys would trim every inch of this small space.

Then I rifled through my stack of vinyl record albums. Wayne had the tape deck and cassettes, but I had my old college turntable. Flipping past each album, I found what I needed: an old LP by The Chipmunks.

I made sure the silly music was playing when the boys arrived. They remembered every word as we sang off-key to the squealing voices of Alvin, Simon, and Theodore. We glued streamers of paper chains and swung them around, dancing about.

After opening their presents, the boys and I headed the three hours to my parents' place in Detroit. I had traveled this route as a single mom several times already. The closer I got to Northville the greater my frozen stomach tension grew. I was plowing into an iceberg named Mom.

Until my deceitful behavior, it was my older brother, Gregg, who upset Mom, one time drunk at sixteen, later protesting the Viet Nam War. However, my divorce was the most devastating for her. Yet as distraught as my conduct made her, the love and devotion she had for the boys never wavered.

When we opened the door and shouted "Merry Christmas!" Mom's kitchen brimmed with the scents of almond and vanilla. On the table, Mom had a freshly baked batch of sugar cookies for the boys to frost.

Mom bent down and snatched the boys into hugs. While they happily buried into her chest, Mom caught my gaze, and her eyes pierced me with unsaid words.

The boys broke free and quickly perched themselves at the kitchen table, frosting one, and eating it while frosting number two.

Dad came in, gave me a kiss on the cheek, smiled softly, and tousled the boys' mop-tops. His quiet demeanor was expected. Dad had not been the disciplinary figure in my childhood house. Mom kept the order and maintained the rules.

"Hey, Papa," they giggled.

"Thanks for this," I said to Mom, nodding to the cookies.

Instead of a simple reply to my thanks, she turned away from the scene and went into the living room. The boys had their heads buried in sugar heaven to finish their frosting project, but I had a clear view and watched Mom pace in a tight circle.

To give Mom some space, I thought it best to offer the boys another activity. "Hey, guys, how about exploring Papa's workshop?"

"Let's build a haunted house like last time," Brian cried out as he slid off his chair.

Mom's head turned at that, and she stepped back into the kitchen. "But it's Christmas," she said, clipping the words into short syllables.

"That's not a problem, Grandma," Adam said. "We celebrate holidays more than once now."

"Yeah, not just here, but at Dad's and Mom's, and Grandma Carol's, too," Brian said. "It's much more fun!"

The boys scurried downstairs, oblivious to the ugly tension filling the space between Mom and me.

With the boys downstairs, I began cleanup while Mom began venting. "This isn't right the way you've left them."

"But Mom, I was so unhappy ..."

"You think it was easy for me? It certainly wasn't. But that's not for you, is it? You just leave and let the rest of us wade through your mess." Her tone sharp, then just as quickly, she sighed and slumped as if there wasn't any fight left in her.

"What's wrong with girls today?" Her voice was almost a whisper.

Mom wasn't looking for an answer, at least not the one I could give her. I nodded and stayed quiet. Things remained peaceful that way. Her venting was a release for her.

She stepped into the pantry, giving me a moment with my thoughts. I was another statistic in a new kind of failure. The mid 1980s saw a skyrocketing divorce rate in the U.S., escalating as high as 65 percent. In Mom's generation the rate hovered at 20 percent. Although I was at the peak of the bell curve, it offered no comfort. I knew that the heartache divorce created was universal, no matter where you fell on the chart.

A crash from the workshop echoed up the basement stairwell. "I'll go check on the boys."

Relieved to get some space between us, I darted downstairs and found the makings of a haunted house.

"Over here, Mom." Adam snagged my hand and tugged me behind a sheet pinned to an indoor clothesline. "Close your eyes."

With my eye covered, I felt a tickle on my face. "Eek!" I screeched and popped my eyes open. A tickly feather was floating from a string looped over the rafters. Brian was pulling the string from behind the other side of the sheet. Giggles erupted.

"Help us finish the rest of the tricks," Brian said. "Then we'll spook Grandma and Papa."

The rest of the weekend passed uneventfully. Castle Grayskull, the fortress the boys coveted for their Masters of the Universe super heroes, became the hit Christmas present for the boys. As they created adventures with He-Man action figures, Mom and I had our own silent stage.

Chapter 18
Big Decision

Celebrating in the new year with Robert, my internal bell rang with glee. Then a few days later as we snuggled on his sofa, he brought up the generous offer outstanding in Bismarck.

"What do you think?" He implored in a serious tone.

I told myself not to do it, but tears fell in an instant, spilling out years of emotions. I hadn't realized how close to the surface my wounds were from the snide remarks all around town. *But could I actually move away?* The idea had such appeal, yet it was such a trade-off.

"It's so far away from the boys." The words rang raw and raspy.

"I'll take care of you." Robert pulled me closer to his chest. His neatly starched shirt barely absorbed my tears. I wiped the rest of them away with the back of my hand.

Although still seated in the soft folds of the sofa, I froze in place, yet feeling so much on the inside. Remembering so much. Ever since the boys were babies, I felt like I had been relentlessly pushing that proverbial boulder uphill. Sitting by my side, Robert shouldered the burden, embraced my flaws, and didn't ignore them.

"Hey." His hand came up and he lifted my chin. "I want to

93

get away from *this*."

His scowl told me he was referring to the barrage of hushed conversations of disapproval.

"It's such a big step." I shifted on the couch.

He bit his lip in thought, and then pushed on. "I want a fresh start. Will you come with me?" He slid his palm from my chin and caressed my cheek. I closed my eyes, letting his hand linger. His touch calmed my racing heart.

"It's so far away from my sons."

"But the offer is enough to provide as many airplane tickets as you need." He let a long silence hang in the air and then drew in a breath. "Well?"

Once again I was a goner for his smooth mellow voice. I took the enormous leap. "I'll move."

Robert's face broke into a big grin. I thought he was going to kiss me, but he lifted me up and tossed me back into the soft folds of the sofa. "So ... I've got something for you. I'll be right back!"

He darted to the front closet and returned with an envelope and a big box. I peeled back the flap of the envelope and slipped out a bundle of Northwest Orient airline tickets. There were hundreds of dollars of gift tickets. "To fly back and forth to see the boys."

"Why didn't you show me these earlier?"

"I thought they'd seem like a bribe. I wanted a true answer."

I started to crumble. He slipped an arm around my shoulder to keep me upright as I wiped at my watery eyes.

"You better let me hold these," he offered. From my happy tears, already a trace of blue appeared on my fingers from the moistened airline carbon paper.

"Now open this." He handed me the box.

I slid off the bow. The red foil paper unfolded and a white box lay underneath. I lifted the hinged top and choked. Robert sprang into action and lifted a white fox fur coat. "Try it on! It's for your first North Dakota winter!"

I snuggled into the feather-light tuft as the collar tickled my chin. "What if I had said no?"

"I figured the coat would be yours no matter what and the tickets can be exchanged for another trip. It just seemed like the right thing to do. Besides, who doesn't need a fur coat in the winter?" Robert's hand came up and curled softly around the back of my neck, bringing his mouth toward mine.

After the kiss, I leaned against his chest for support, "How will I tell the boys?" My voice sounded weak and wobbly.

"It won't be easy."

"I'm terrified. I don't feel brave enough."

"Being brave doesn't mean you're not scared. It's being scared and doing it anyway – to be free to start fresh." His words were soft, his thoughts sincere. He wrapped his arms around me and I held on tight.

Chapter 19

Hardest Day of My Life

Wayne opened and shut his mouth. Stared hard at me, looked away from me. Gnawed on his inner cheek, moistened his lips.

"Moving? To North Dakota? Abandoning the boys!"

"No, I'll be back in three weeks. And I'll take the boys to my parents for winter break just like we planned." I rattled off the words as fast as I could; afraid if I didn't they would never come out.

"Then what? You won't be making Tuesday night commitments. Oh! That's right. You always want to change Tuesdays, anyway."

I held on, in my mind, to Robert's earlier words. Be brave.

I ignored the Tuesday comment and said, "After winter break I want to schedule monthly visits."

"You're going to jaunt back from Bismarck, North Dakota, once a month? Oh, I get it. The doctor is going to share his money. Isn't that easy!"

I passed over that remark, too.

"I want to have the kids for a week. On the weekend, I'll

take them to visit my folks, but on school days we can stay at the Rest Easy. I'll get them to school and maintain their regular schedule."

"You'll 'maintain their regular schedule,' huh?" he said, flashing air quotes with his fingers. "Tell me one thing about this plan of yours that is 'regular.'"

"It's the same visitation amount. Just in a different format."

"Different format?" He paced the room in circles. "You waltz in here and throw this at me. I can't believe it. No, wait, I can believe it. You've been thoughtless since this chaos started."

All the bones in my body collapsed as guilt flowed through me, yet somehow I pressed on. "I have twenty-five percent visitation times."

"What you have is irresponsibility, Kathy." He stopped moving and his eyes pierced through to my marrow. "What happened to the girl I married? Oh, yeah, she left."

We stared at each other for a moment. Wayne had gotten very still. I'm not sure he was even breathing.

"You know what? Your visits disrupt our routine no matter when you pick the boys up. Just go." His voice became as limp as his frame.

With my head down, I left. Flight was easier; I was weak.

Next I called Mom.

"I'll have your dad come talk to you." That was all she said to me.

Dad drove three hours from Detroit to come "talk" to me. As I tugged open the door to the Bill Knapp's restaurant where I was meeting him, a chill hunted every gap in my coat, but it wasn't from the January cold. Right away, I spied his listless frame slumped in a booth. The clatter of dishes and the buzz of background conversations vanished, leaving my head in a muffled mess as the magnitude of what I had to say hit me. I took a seat across from him.

He couldn't even meet my eyes. He clutched a cup of coffee that had sat untouched for so long a black ring had formed at the top. "Your mother is too upset to talk." He shifted in his seat, coughed behind his hand, and then hung his head, staying quiet. He'd driven three hours, but could only say those seven words.

"I love you, Dad. Mom, too. Robert makes me happier than I've ever been. I'm so sorry."

He nodded and then stood, giving me a hug. I held him as tight as I could. It was the most difficult visit I'd ever had with him.

Then I had to tell the boys.

I paced and felt my chest tighten again, with a different kind of fierceness. It was the intense love for my sons and concern about this talk. Standing outdoors at our apartment complex, I watched them playing on the jungle gym. I took a deep breath to steady my nerves and called them over. I snatched them into a hug and inhaled that fresh-from-the-playground sweaty scent.

Brian wriggled free first, which was the norm. He tended to be less comfortable with outward signs of affection, internalizing by instinct and usually not giving anything away until we sat silently for a good ten minutes. In fact, it took fifteen minutes during our last visit for him to tell me that he hadn't made starting sweeper on his soccer team. I worried about him in a way I didn't Adam, whose spontaneous nature allowed his emotions to be out there for the world to see.

I pulled Brian back into our huddle, my heart drilling hard in my chest.

"I'm moving to a new place, but I'll be back in three Fridays, just a little longer than most times we're together." I placed a hand on each of their hearts. "I know it's sad. But remember what it feels like in here." I tapped on their chests like a soft heartbeat. "Remember how it feels so good when we hug, and laugh, and have funny-face contests." I paused and swallowed the thickness in my throat. "Well, to feel all that good, and that happy, we need to know how to feel sad, too. Otherwise we can't feel happy. So it's okay to feel sad about this. While I'm gone just remember that I'm always, always, in here." I tapped their hearts one more time.

"Is there a playground at the new place?" Adam asked.

"Yes, there's a playground."

The boys gave me an extra big squeeze, and I gave a silent thanks to the counselor I'd continued to visit. He coached me to simplify this conversation to the boys' level of understanding. Only moments later, they raced to climb into the Chevette and I trailed behind, wiping my tears away before they could see them.

In the months ahead, it was a smooth change for them. Not such a smooth change for me.

Chapter 20

A Fresh Start

The move to Bismarck unfolded uneventfully. On the January target date, a crew of packers came and had both our places boxed and loaded in a day.

We slid out of Michigan in slushy January snow and eventually rolled across the North Dakota border with the sun shimmering in the brightest blue sky I had ever seen. The hum of the tires rolling along I-94 had me daydreaming about the condo we had selected and Robert had purchased for our new home. My thoughts drifted back to a couple of weeks earlier when we studied photographs of condos and narrowed our interest down to one.

"This is a nice one," Robert had remarked about the finalist. "It's brand new, with a fireplace in the master suite, an indoor hot tub, and look at this!" Robert waved a photo of a drywalled lower level. "You can have your own art studio."

My heart raced as I studied that photograph. The space was huge! It would be like moving from a walk-in closet to a tennis court. "It'd be perfect," I agreed.

I had flipped through the pictures one more time, awe-struck at the contemporary feel of high ceilings and sharp angles. "This is a great space for your piano." I pointed to a room filled with floor to ceiling windows.

"I'll call and inquire about the details. I can ask to have your studio painted and carpeted before we arrive."

Suddenly we hit a bump on the interstate and the jerky motion shook me out of my reverie. The flat prairie seemed to stretch endlessly as we passed mile after mile on the road trip to our new home.

"We're getting closer. Probably less than half an hour away." Robert placed his hand over mine and that familiar tingle raced through me.

Finally we pulled up to the condo. It was perched along a high ridge, with the glistening Missouri River flowing far below. The air floating up was cool and misty, making every breath I took fresher, cleaner, and a bit magical.

Settling in was our own kind of honeymoon. The movers had arrived ahead and unpacked all but a few personal boxes. I had moved many times in my life, but never with this kind of white-glove service.

Robert started his new job and, as planned, my first goal was to help him set up his office. I ordered all his favorites: a special brand of Silvadene cream for burns, distinct finger splints, newborn head calipers, and much, much more. A mere two weeks into his new practice, and his office needs were well organized. Then it was time for me to look for a job. An art-related job, as we had discussed!

Getting out the Yellow Pages, I scanned the business sections. A quarter-page ad promoted an award-winning advertising agency. I had enjoyed designing the brochure for Robert's med center and the style for our Christmas card. *Maybe my art could fit into the mix of graphic design?* I dialed the number and chatted my way into an appointment to meet the owner.

Just over a week later, in mid-February, I stepped out nervously into the frigid Bismarck weather clutching my art presentation case feeling as chilly on the inside. Showing my art was like exposing my soul!

Entering the reception area of Serig Advertising, I edged into a seat. An intercom buzzed and the receptionist rose from a nearby desk, squaring the shoulders of her business blazer. I had on a similar suit, but I wasn't dressed with half her confidence. "Mr. Serig will see you now."

I rose and shook off my nerves.

When I walked into the office, Bill Serig reached across his desk and gave me the classic two-handed North Dakota handshake I had grown accustomed to since our first visit. He wore a trimmed beard, and his eyes were creased behind the thick lenses of his square glasses. He was short but his voice was big. "Have a seat and show me what ya got."

I laid out my portfolio on his desk and sank into a seat opposite him, pressing my palms firmly against my skirt to keep my legs from shaking.

Finally he finished viewing my samples. "Beautiful. But you're too 'fine art' for an advertising agency. I'd focus on that skill if I were you."

Thanking him for his time and friendly professional assessment, I scurried out of his office a bit disappointed even though I knew I didn't have any formal training in the mechanics of graphic design layout.

That night I shared my experience with Robert and he asked, "So how do you focus on your fine art?"

"Well, I'm not sure. He's suggesting I concentrate on my

watercolors, but there aren't any retail galleries in Bismarck for me to sell my paintings."

He nodded in agreement.

"But there is the Bismarck Art and Gallery Association. I can check on the possibility of booking an art show. But they usually schedule exhibits way in advance."

"What other ideas do you have?"

"Well, I've been scouring the Help Wanted ads. One caught my eye. A department store has an opening in sales for custom drapery. With my sewing background, maybe it'll be intriguing. I've always liked mixing fabric colors together. Maybe I'll be able to design different styles of valances, pinch pleats, Roman shades ..." My list trailed off.

"That's sounds interesting. I'd follow up on that."

"Sure thing." I assumed Robert's concern about me finding a job was driven by his support for me and my newly found passion in the world of art, so when the oven timer buzzed, I busied myself serving dinner.

The next day I followed up on the drapery job at the Montgomery Ward store and interviewed later the next week. They offered me the position, and that night I told Robert the news. "It's selling door-to-door using a catalog," I reported. "There are only a dozen color choices and two styles of drapes. Turns out the only thing 'custom' about it is adjusting the size to fit their window."

"Does that make it a bad job?"

I was a little puzzled. Robert and I had spent months talking about how watercolor brought me a challenge that I had not found in the rote work of crafts and in the routine of checking vital signs.

"Well, it's not the variety I was hoping for," I said. "And it only pays two-fifty an hour." I gave a little laugh. "At Christmas I paid two dollars an hour for a high schooler to babysit so I told them I wasn't interested."

"Can you afford to turn down the job?"

I didn't expect to hear that answer.

Assuming that I had misunderstood his reaction, I presented an idea that I was sure would delight Robert. "I want to create a presentation for St. Alexius' pediatric remodeling project." St. Alexius was the hospital that employed Robert. "With my nursing background, I think I can do a good job. I'll create paintings to match animated wallpaper borders. That'll add color for the kids yet maintain the plain white walls you doctors need for evaluating patient pallor while they're hospitalized."

"Is that your only lead for a job?" he asked.

I thought he would be excited about this new idea. *Where was his enthusiasm for my art?* I was perplexed. Maybe he just couldn't picture the project yet. "Wait until you see my sketches; that'll clarify the concept."

"Well, I'll feel more comfortable when you have a job." His expression was unreadable.

I felt confused. After all, he built a huge studio for me. Maybe he thought I wasn't serious about working since I had turned down today's offer. "I'll keep looking; you know I like to keep busy. We always planned I'd work, but in the meantime I'll draw out the pediatric concept for you to see."

He flashed a flicker of a smile – the opposite of his teasing, easy-going grin. In fact, it was so out of character I chalked it up to Robert having a bad day. Any concerns that might have crossed my mind were chased away by my own enthusiasm for this marketing idea.

In my art studio, one idea quickly led to the next. I created Alex the Cat, a mascot for St. Alexius, who cared "purr-fectly" for every little kid. In addition to the wallpaper borders and coordinating watercolor for each children's room, I added Alex frolicking in paintings for the main corridor.

As my enthusiasm grew, my pencil had wings and flew across the paper. I had one idea after another ... coloring books that made it easy and fun for ailing kids to understand and learn about their hospital stay ... a bravery badge to pin on the tykes ... I even sketched an adult-size costume of Alex to kick up his heels when he marched in the Fourth of July Parade!

Although confident that I nailed a top-notch concept, I knew I was headed into uncharted territory. In the late 1980s, medical ethics reigned, and marketing a hospital was virtually a new concept. I was determined, though, and embraced the idea at full throttle.

Another innovation emerged. The hospital could publish a newsletter to inform parents of the pediatric patients about its services. I drew Alex into a headline and added paw prints for the newsletter border.

Over the next couple of days, I jotted down even more ideas. It would take me some time to refine the concepts and visual aids for the marketing campaign. First, I had to hop on a plane to go see the boys!

*On left, one of the corridor art pieces featured on St.
Alexius annual report. On right, one of two coloring books*

Chapter 21
Much Needed Hugs

The airliner hit a cruising speed of 540 mile per hour, and for me, that wasn't fast enough. After being away from my sons for three weeks, I couldn't wait to scoop up and hug them for February winter break. I toted in my carry-on a Nintendo game console they would flip over. It was a winter replacement for a playground.

When I arrived, the boys had a week of school remaining before winter break began, so I checked into the Rest Easy motel, a string of eight single rooms, with a microwave and pint-size fridge, to get the room organized for their stay with me.

As the visit began, we settled right in to our days together. Time raced by as I shared the rhythms of my sons' lives: homework, brotherly bickering, running late ... and the fun times, like when I picked them up after school in the rental car jam-packed with balloons. I had blown up hundreds as part of a birthday celebration. I was grateful for every second we shared.

At the end of the week on Friday, we rolled out of West Michigan with the sky as sunny as our moods. By the time we got to my parents' house in the Detroit area, the sky was a sea of gray, and just as the boys raced to the door, the snowstorm began.

Mom wrestled them into a hug. "I ordered the flakes especially for your visit!"

Giggling and kicking off winter boots, they announced big plans: "We're heading downstairs. We've thought up new tricks for another haunted house!"

They zoomed off, and I soon heard my dad's hearty laugh echo up from his workshop as he greeted them.

"Thanks for having us, Mom."

"I can't believe you moved so far away."

I had heard these same words over the phone. "I'm sorry, Mom. "It's just ..."

Mom pressed on, "At least Wayne has some sense, always keeping the boys first. But not you. You don't just leave ... you move! All for a promise. A promise of what?"

"I trust what I feel for Robert."

"Well, I would have never gone without being married. After all, *That Man* didn't marry you," she said, refusing to use Robert's name.

I flinched at that, and then felt myself wither.

Mom continued, "I thought I taught you to believe in wedding vows. But it turns out they don't mean anything to you so I guess it doesn't matter."

Mom's philosophy of marriage had nurtured her. Instead of getting upset about her views, I understood her reaction as the result of her own upbringing and family history.

"I'll unload the car," I said, finding it easier to skate away.

Out in the crisp winter air, the heat in my cheeks faded. I watched the falling flakes. "Angel feathers," I said to myself. "That's what the boys call the snow." Thinking of my sons made me want to smile and cry at the same time. This mix of emotions tugged at me daily in my role as a single mom. Although my time with the boys was shorter, there was a quality in my ability to nurture them. I took in a lungful of the chilly fresh air. Primarily because of Robert, I could breathe with relief and relish this time with my sons. I felt the snow was feathers from the wings of an angel watching over me.

By morning the winter winds had piled a huge snowdrift across the front entrance to my parent's condo. The boys and I wrapped up in winter garb, created snow tunnels, and snaked through it all, wriggling and giggling the entire time.

That night I called Robert to share my happiness. The phone rang and rang. That was odd. Robert was on call for emergencies that week, which meant he wouldn't stray far from the telephone. I tried later in the evening, but still no answer.

The next night, Scott picked up.

Scott? He was a neighbor we had met at Robert's first condo, back in Michigan. He had become a mutual friend ... but what was he doing in Bismarck?

"Just visiting" was the answer Robert gave when he finally came to the phone.

I shrugged it off, but the moment lodged, unsettled, in a corner of my mind.

The remainder of the Detroit visit flew by. While I packed the car, thunder boomed in the sky and then a wintry rain hammered onto our snow fort. I bolted back to the condo from the driveway.

"Looks like this storm is going to wash away all your fun," Dad said to his grandsons.

"At least it held off till now," Adam said. "We've got school tomorrow, anyhow."

I marveled at the way the boys found the bright side of things.

A few hours later, back out front of the Colonial, we said our goodbyes. Sadness tugged at my heart and I shook like the quivering leaves of a birch tree. I could see the boys again in three weeks and four days. Until then, I clung to thoughts of returning to Robert. Only he could ease my agony.

And he did. At the airport he stood like a mighty oak, spreading his arms wide and powerfully wrapping me in his strength.

* * *

After several weeks of preparing, I had a mascot, I had coloring books, and interior color designs for the renovation project at the St. Alexius pediatric unit. I was ready to present my colorful creations. But to whom would I make a pitch?

My finger traced the listings of the hospital directory. Knowing that there wasn't an advertising department, per se, I searched for related entities such as public relations or community services. It turned out neither of those departments could help me. Then I tried Human Resources, thinking its employees might listen to my spiel about the St. Alexius "customer," aka patient.

A gruff voice responded to my phone pitch. "We service the employees. But you mentioned color; I'll connect you to another department." Transferred to the Audio-Visual Department, I presented my idea once again.

"Sorry, I'm just the slide projector guy."

Click.

I kept dialing. Finally, I got an appointment with the facilities manager. I wasn't certain what his role involved, but I was excited to add the appointment to my calendar in big bold letters. It was a start, after all.

In between my creative bursts for the pediatric wing, pleasant social times emerged with Robert and his professional crowd. For one special event we hosted, I sautéed, sizzled, and savored in the kitchen, preparing a five-course meal for four of Robert's physician friends and their wives.

In the dining room I set an elegant dinner table, including swan folded linen napkins. Per Robert's idea, in the loft on a second dining table for the event, I set everyone's dessert plates, topped with cup and saucers for coffee alongside crystal brandy snifters.

All during the special evening, Robert passed me his warm smile and let out his rich laugh often. The laugh that made me join in ... every time. Any mixed messages I might have sensed regarding my job hunting evaporated.

Chapter 22

This Wasn't Happening

Zoom. The next trip to see my sons went well, flew right by, and I was headed back to Bismarck. On descent, the plane slapped the ground with a thud and then rumbled over patches of icy snow on the runway. I felt as frigid on the inside as I knew I had to wait three weeks before I saw the boys again.

With my luggage gathered, I wrapped my winter coat collar high around my neck against the bitter March wind, then I fought my way to long-term parking. Crossing the icy lot, Robert's earlier idea for me to park the Chevette at the airport ran through my mind.

"I might go out of town for a day while you're gone," he said.

"Any place in particular?" Curiosity stirred in me, as we had yet to travel much outside the city since moving to Bismarck almost three months ago.

"Maybe just explore some old Western culture, eat a buffalo burger or two. Just in case I'm running late, you'll have your car handy."

As I crawled inside the frozen Chevette, the vinyl seat crackled like ice cubes. I cranked the engine over and cold air from the dashboard vents hit me in the face.

Halfway home, heated air finally swarmed around me. Not just from the car heater, but from reading the movie arcade. *Pretty Woman* flashed in lights. Richard Gere was Julia Roberts' Prince Charming, Robert was mine. I couldn't wait to be in Robert's arms, so I gave the gas pedal an extra pump.

Before I hit the garage door opener, the *Check Engine* light flashed red in my face. I inched the little hatchback into the garage just as a cloud of steam hissed from under the hood. Even I knew this didn't look good, but I pushed aside my car troubles thinking I didn't have to tackle them until morning. Tonight I longed for a quiet evening in front of the fireplace with Robert.

Leaving the car to cool off, I found Robert in the loft, hunched over his baby grand piano, playing a powerful baritone Beethoven. He didn't look up when I entered the room. Something was amiss.

"What's wrong?"

He stopped playing. His eyes avoided me, staying focused on the idle keyboard. The instant I saw no ring on his finger, I was worried.

Robert raised his eyes to me. However, the sparkle that usually glowed was gone. I clasped my hands to my chest, fondled my own aquamarine promise ring and stood speechless. Instantly, he knew I had noticed his missing band.

"The ring was like a noose." He rubbed at the shadow line on his bare finger as if he were wishing he could erode the mark away. "I was feeling strangled." His voice was cold and direct, knocking the air out of my lungs.

"But the rings were your idea."

"I know, I know." He shifted uncomfortably on the piano bench.

This wasn't making any sense. "What's happened? Everything seemed fine when I left."

He nodded, and then hung his head.

"Then what have I done wrong?"

He pushed out a heavy sigh. "You've done nothing wrong." He rubbed the back of his neck with his hand.

"Then what is it?"

"I'm just unsure about some things."

"Unsure?" I was having difficulty making any sense of this sudden change in Robert's demeanor. He was the man who made precise, split-second medical decisions. He was the man who didn't hesitate to enjoy his passion in art and music. He was the man who promised us a life together.

"Things happened so fast."

Fast? This move to Bismarck was his idea. I couldn't wrap my mind around the whirlwind in my head.

"This isn't working," he said, waving an arm around the room we had decorated together.

Robert's words whirled around me, out of focus. I sunk into the couch. So many questions spun around in my mind. I couldn't even land on one.

He shifted again on the piano bench, this time pushing himself upright. Although he stood over me, he seemed small. "Just give me some time alone ..." his voice a harsh whisper as he walked out of the room.

I found myself rocking side to side, like a mother's habit to calm her baby.

What was happening? Give him time alone?

Trance-like, I made my way to the lower level art studio and began pushing papers around to avoid the situation for a few moments.

Then, a while later, Robert's footsteps announced he was descending the stairs. "Maybe you should consider nursing instead of that project." The St. Alexius project laid in a sprawl around me.

Even though his words came at me from behind, they hit me square in the chest. "I thought you believed in my artistic talent?" My voice sounded as raw as my throat felt.

"It's just that I'd feel more comfortable if you had a real job."

"But this interview has the potential to provide me with income for a year," I said, hoping it would remind him about how extensive my ideas were for the hospital. "Why suddenly is my art not good enough?"

"Your art is good. It's just ... I'm worried if it's enough."

"Enough?" I couldn't wrap my mind around these strange requests. Robert looked the same but he wasn't acting the same.

"That was before you were on your own," he said. "Now, you'll need steady income you can count on."

My heart pounded in my ears.

"On ... my ... own?" I could hardly form the words. "I don't understand. Did something happen when I was gone?" I grabbed at anything, something that might give me an answer.

"No, nothing happened. I just need some time to think."

The room began to spin. I stumbled to a chair and collapsed. My heart thumped in my throat and echoed in my ears. No longer could I fight the emotions. It was more than

I could hold on to. I hid my face, but I couldn't keep my shoulders from shaking. I fought off the hot tears trying to convince myself that this was like a bad paint spill, one that could be wiped away, leaving no trace of the words Robert had uttered.

Robert slipped out of the studio. In a daze I gathered the remaining samples into my presentation case. I was too numb, too confused to be angry. All I could do was pray that by the time I got upstairs this nightmare would be end.

However, when I shuffled from the art studio, things weren't at all what I hoped. Robert had the door to the guest room closed. *What's going on? This can't be happening.* In my state of disbelief, a sob crept up my throat, burst into the air, and all the tears I had been trying not to shed erupted.

I crawled into our bed, under cold sheets, and huddled under a layer of blankets and wrapped myself in a bundle of denial. *Things will be different in the morning. Robert will be the Robert who promised me the world.*

Chapter 23
Denial

After an endless night, the only sound I heard in the morning was the wind eerily whistling through the fireplace flue in the master suite. Somehow, Robert had slipped out. He must have gathered a change of clothes when I was in the art studio last night.

I limped into the shower and sobbed. It wasn't until the hot water turned frigid that I forced myself to get out. Somehow, through my stunned state, I heard the clock chime eight and my mind finally focused. I had the St. Alexius marketing meeting this morning. The meeting I had prepared for weeks.

Right away, I had to pull myself together; it was simply too late to cancel. I represented not just myself, but Robert as well. It was his hospital. And "we" were supposed to be building a future with them and this town. I convinced myself that if I could land the design contract that day. Then Robert would really admire my artistic skills and our relationship would be back on track by dinnertime.

Selecting my best business suit – a gift from Robert – I hoped the fine cashmere might cloak me in the confidence that had been stripped away the night before.

It wasn't until I stepped into the garage that I remembered the Chevette check engine light! It seemed like weeks earlier that steam had been sizzling from the engine. I held my breath and turned the key in the ignition. The Chevette sputtered to life, and the *Check Engine* light stayed off. I took the absence of a red light as a good omen and nursed the little car the short distance to St. Alexius.

After parking, I gathered my portfolio. In our phone conversation, Bert Stahl, the hospital facility manager, directed me to follow the color-coded arrows in the building. Descending to the basement, I turned the corner to find Stahl, dressed in a crisp brown uniform, seated at an industrial desk, his broad frame overpowering it.

He nodded at me after I introduced myself. "You can begin your pitch," he said, his gruff voice unsettling my already frazzled nerves.

Halfway through my presentation he held up his hand like a *STOP* sign. "You need to see Glen Beckman, the hospital administrator." He picked up the phone, croaked out a few sentences, hung up, and gave me directions.

Upstairs the administrator's assistant greeted me and straight away, she ushered me into Mr. Beckman's office. With an unreadable face, Mr. Beckman sat through the proposal. Then he simply got up and walked right out of the room.

A minute passed. Three minutes. It felt like an eternity. A terrified knocking in my rib cage kept me company. What was going on? I wondered.

An adjoining door finally swung open. "I went to get Mr. Snider, the Dean of the Hospital." Mr. Beckman stepped aside and the head honcho of St. Alexius' 306-bed acute-care medical facility filled the room.

Mr. Snider's dark eyes were guarded and gave nothing away. "Glen told me the concept. I'm impressed, but we've already hired the architect."

My spirits started to plummet, but he continued, "However, we certainly can approve that lovable Alex as the mascot for coloring books and paintings in the pediatric unit. But you'll need to get the architect's approval for the interior designs."

I did an internal dance of glee; I'd landed part of my first art job with good money! I just had that final hurdle to clear with the architect.

On the way out the door, I bumped into the facility manager again.

"How'd your meeting go?" Mr. Stahl asked in his gruff tone.

"Okay. It went okay," I forced a stiff smile.

"I knew it was a grand concept," he said, showing the beginnings of a grin. "You have a mighty fine talent, but I'm the fix-it guy around here, not the art guy."

Fix-It Guy, I repeated to myself, thinking about the Chevette's warning light. "Do you know anyone who works on older cars?"

Mr. Stahl made a quick call and sent me to his neighbor's second-cousin, a guy named Mark. By noon, the Chevette purred once again.

The total repair took a hefty dent out of my small savings, but rather than worry about that, I happily steered the repaired Chevette toward home. I couldn't wait to tell Robert the art news because I was certain it would make the craziness disappear.

Chapter 24

Trying Hard –
Plan B, Plan C

Hope was ticking its way around the face of the clock in the kitchen as I prepared a special meal for Robert. By the time he strolled in, beef stroganoff had been slowly simmering for an hour, and the yeasty smell of homemade dinner rolls had begun to fill the room.

With his tight jaw and stern stare, I realized that preparing his favorite food had failed. Then his words confirmed it.

"I'm sorry, but this isn't going to work." He waved to the table that I'd set for two. "I need some space and time to think."

"I can give you space." I took a few steps back to show I could be supportive. I'd walk to the ends of the Earth to make this all go away.

"I mean I need you to look for another place to live."

What? Where was this coming from? "You want me to do what?"

His shoulders stiffened with the rising tension. "Look for a place. Yes. That would be best."

Trying to make sense of what he was saying, I pushed

through the chaos in my head. "But you promised us a life together."

"I did." He dropped his head. "It's just ... things are different here than I expected."

"What do you mean by different?"

"I can't put my finger on it. That's what I need time to think about."

My face grew hot as I got more confused. "How can things *not* be as you expected? I've done everything you asked. I set up your office. I entertain your friends, I run all the errands, I even got a job today!" I hadn't wanted to share my exciting news this way, but I was in survival mode, fighting to negotiate some kind of truce.

"Just stop!"

The ugly punch of his tone hit me hard and I gasped.

He paused for a moment. "Look, I'm sorry, but please don't fight me on this. Let's just try it. You just need to make a plan, and then work through the steps ..."

His words slammed into me and rocked me backward on my heels like a blast of wind. Robert had coached me with those exact same words when I left Wayne and the boys! *If you make a list of all the steps you need to do it'll keep you from thinking about all the ways you could fall apart.*

It's the most pain that I'd known in my life. My breath jammed into my lungs. I sucked in a lungful of air, thrust my chin up, and this time yelled it right out: "Then why did you move me out here?!!"

His face offered no clues. He stood there like stone and let me shout.

I couldn't stop, either. "Why? Why! Why?"

Finally my roar became raw. Then, as quickly as the hot

anger had risen, I found myself crumbling into a heap and breaking into sobs.

"Look. I don't have any answers today. Let me sort out a few things." Robert's feet shifted, turning away. "I'll grab something to eat in town."

That was it from him; nothing more.

Moments later I heard the soft click of the door closing, but it echoed like thunder. I don't know how long I stayed slumped there in one spot ... the same questions running through my mind: *Why did he want me in Michigan, and now not here? What is different here that made him change his mind about us? About me?*

I didn't have one answer.

Darkness surrounded me and hours passed. Numbly, I limped to bed. All night I faced the horror of it all when I rolled over and remembered Robert wasn't there.

The next morning when I heard the shower attached to the guest bedroom running, I realized he had come home sometime during my restless sleep. Once the water ended, his footsteps padded on the stairs leading to our room. He needed fresh work clothes.

Not brave enough to face him, I hid under the blanket and uttered, "I can try harder to make this work."

"I know you're willing, but I'm confused about a lot of things."

"I don't understand." I moved the blanket off my face. It wasn't protecting me from the gut-wrenching agony of his words anyway.

"I don't really, either." His voice was a half-whisper. Grave.

"Mr. Snider approved my marketing plan," I blurted out,

name dropping the hospital dean, thinking maybe he hadn't heard me the previous night. "I got the job you were asking me about before I visited the boys. I'll be meeting with the architect in charge."

"You're a good artist. But take the first step and look for a place to live, please." His words had a pleading ring.

The door snapped shut, leaving me with more unanswered questions: Wouldn't he miss our evenings sipping Pinot Grigio, our walks in the rain, our laughing over Gilbert and Sullivan? As I lay in bed, Robert's words replayed in my mind, including the ones that had lured me away from life at the Colonial: *"Embrace yourself. Be who you are, not what others want or expect."*

I sat up, determined to continue supporting Robert. He had supported me, after all. I would look for a place to live, and he would discover he missed me, and any minute he would crave all the things we had in common. I was certain we'd reunite. The next day. Next week. Next month, at the latest.

My confidence lasted about as long as my shower. What if we didn't reconcile? I felt my cheeks prick with heat, realizing my other option was to move back to Michigan. My thoughts shifted to my mom. From the beginning she'd insisted I shouldn't leave Michigan. She thought I should stick it out with my marriage. Like she did.

Like clockwork, guilt and shame soon washed over me. I was too humiliated to utter one word to Mom about this trouble. Therefore, I responded in the only way my cowardice would allow. I decided to try Robert's plan of "taking a break."

I crawled out of bed and searched the phone book for the

number of Dan Duran, the architect. He was the professional who needed to approve my plan before I began the pediatric wing interior selections and art. After dialing, I cleared my throat, trying to control the tremor in my voice.

A stern female voice answered. In a rush, I rattled off my situation.

"We're a very busy office." Her words clipped short.

My whole relationship with Robert depended on this job. I had to make him proud of me. Then things would be back to normal. I needed this job. "Excuse me, but Mister Snider, the dean of the Hospital, asked that I speak to Dan Duran in this matter."

That apparently did the trick; I got the appointment!

Chapter 25

Home Isn't Where the Heart Is

From the street curb, 715 North Second Street looked unremarkable. However, staring at this tired-looking three-story house was remarkable. Having been in Bismarck for barely three months, I had to seek a new place to live. My breath caught high in my chest. I forced out a sigh, and then trudged up the front steps. As I stood on the small stoop in a city neighborhood of older homes packed side by side, I pushed out another long sigh and then pressed the doorbell.

The old wooden door opened and, not surprisingly, it creaked with age. There stood a short woman with a headful of gray curls and a face that looked as weathered as the door. "Come in, come in."

Toasty warm air swallowed me up as I stepped inside. Then an enormous jungle cat arched his back at me and thrust his tail straight into the air.

"That's Butterscotch, my precious," the old lady stated with pride about the huge house cat. "Don't mind him. It takes time for Butterscotch to warm up to new folks. So, dear, my name is Marge. Marge Witt." Her voice softened, unlike the cat, which was making unsettling howling noises deep in his throat. "I've cleaned out my mother's apartment, bless her soul, so let's go take a look."

I recoiled at the thought of viewing a dead lady's former living space, but I followed.

"My husband, Fred, did all the handiwork down there before his passing. I'm taking you down by the way of the side entrance, but your main door is private, through the back of the house."

I didn't really catch a word of what she was saying after hearing that another person had died in this old house. Marge marched down the wooden staircase while I shuffled behind descending to the basement apartment. A lone bare bulb lit the darkness. My feet scuffed across a cold cement floor, then past the furnace, a hot water heater, and unfinished stud walls. I couldn't wrap my mind around it all. *Is this how I'd enter my new home? How would I ever bring art clients here for a meeting?* It couldn't have been more different than the condo.

Marge prattled on as we stepped into a kitchen the size of a coffin. Small narrow windows shed a sliver of light high above my head, reminding me that I was well below ground level.

The old gal had taken three steps to stand in a not-much-larger room. "Come down this way." She motioned me to follow as she moved into a shoebox of a bedroom.

I tasted nausea in my throat, pushed it down, and inched my way forward. The windows were larger here than the teeny kitchen, but the view was of the backside of a shabby shed only a few feet away.

Marge moved a few steps forward and swung open another door, letting in a chilly breeze from the outside. This time her words sunk in. "This is your private entrance." She stood in a long, narrow foyer, and then moved next to me.

"Now let me take a closer look at you. Mm-hmm," she said. "You'll do just fine. I have a way of knowing these things. You'll find my tenants become my family. Just ask Nora, who lives upstairs. She's like a daughter to me."

Marge finished giving me the once over, and then nodded as her mouth slipped into a smile.

Then, from out of nowhere, that bundle of flying fur called Butterscotch suddenly was in my arms and nuzzling me with a lusty purr rumbling from his chest. Heat from his big body seeped into mine and began to warm me.

"I knew Butterscotch would befriend you. So you'll take the apartment?"

The hard truth gnawed at my chest. How could I not? The tiny apartment fit my tiny budget. *Besides*, I convinced myself, *this was temporary.*

* * *

The last thing I wanted was to be living alone in North Dakota. Nevertheless, that's what was happening. Back in the kitchen of the condo, as I stood facing Robert, I clung to the granite counter for support to hold myself upright, hoping that what I had to say would convince him to change his mind. I pulled in a deep breath. "I looked for a place to live."

I searched his face for an expression I might recognize ... the breezy smile, the infectious energy. Instead all I caught were his eyes avoiding me.

"Was there anything available?"

The words crushed all the hope I had that Robert would

tell me he changed his mind and that I could cancel the move. "There's an apartment in a house downtown."

"That's good," he said, just like that. "I'll arrange a truck if you give me an address."

His words hung heavy in the air. This time it was me to look away.

"Look." The quiet way Robert said the word made me raise my head to attention. "I know this is difficult, but let's give this a try. It's the first step; we'll see how it goes."

"But what happened? I still don't understand." I begged with my eyes. I couldn't help myself. These questions had been running a continuous loop like a cassette tape, over and over in my head.

"I don't know. Once we got out here, suddenly I feel freer. It makes me want to explore."

"I thought we wanted the same things like exploring the symphony and trying new foods like German Spätzle smothered in caramelized onions ..." I let my voice trail off, hoping he could picture the moments we had shared.

"We do have similar tastes. It's just I'm unsure of what direction I need to take."

"You mean about your job?"

"Work is fine."

"Then what?" I couldn't make sense of his remarks.

"I don't have an answer. I'm just not certain about things." More evasive words, yet they stung with exactness.

In a desperate act I grabbed onto more fond memories, hoping they might shake Robert into the man I remembered. "What about that autumn trip to Fifty Lakes, when the red maples leaves shimmered in the sun and you bought me the diamond earrings?"

"Yes, we like the finer things in life, but this is something different. I can't explain it."

"Can you try?"

"I have been." His stance stiffened. "I'm sorry. I know I'm not giving you much. I'm not sure what I'm feeling. Maybe it's just a mid-life thing."

Six years older than me, I thought Robert had already been through a mid-life crisis with his divorce. "Back in Michigan, we joked about being each other's mid-life answer," I said, trying to make the words sound light and airy, like the teasing had been at the time.

Robert's jaw muscle twitched, but his lips drew tight instead of into a grin. "Yes, we quipped about that. But now, I'm not sure."

Where were all these self-doubts about us coming from? Anger bounced through me like a pinball, ricocheting through my insides, but I held my tongue.

"I just seem to be finding more questions," he said.

"What kind of questions?"

Waiting for his answer became pure agony as the kitchen clock clawed off painful seconds.

"I'm sorry. You're pushing me in a direction I don't have answers to right now." Robert's sturdy frame folded and he seemed to shrink in front of my eyes. "Please just take the apartment." His voice sounded small.

My anger eased. I loved this man. I believed in us. I would help him through his internal battle doing it his way. I took the apartment.

Two days later through a drizzling rain, I aimed the compact Chevette away from the condo on the ridge and downshifted toward the close quarters of city living. The gray fog grew thicker and shrouded my confused heart.

I parked in front of the old house as the moving truck rumbled into the driveway. Two husky men hoisted the furniture into the pocketsize apartment in no time and then left. Through the spit of sleet, I lugged boxes from the car. To keep my mind from thoughts I didn't want, I hunkered down and unpacked into the wee hours. Luckily, exhaustion from the day pushed me into a restless sleep.

At daybreak, the memory of Robert's request for time apart hit me like a wrecking ball. I squeezed my eyes shut, trying to force my mind to go blank, but it wouldn't. No matter where I stood, where I walked, where I forced my thoughts, the ache of his absence followed me.

Eventually, although in a stoic state, I press forward and prepared for my scheduled appointment with Duran Architects. While I gathered my presentation portfolio, a robin chirped on the windowsill. Its bright red breast blazed against the gray day.

It was my first robin of spring. Praying the sprightly bird was a good omen, I made a wish, convincing myself that if I secured this art contract through the architect, then things could return to the way I imagined with Robert. Happily ever after.

Chapter 26
A Small Victory

Although April was only two weeks away, it was far from being spring in North Dakota. It was merely the end stage of the long northern plains winter. Overnight the temperature had dropped, reverting the walk once again into an ice rink. Not paying enough attention, I took my first step out of the apartment and skidded on the slick cement. The art case sailed into the air, further throwing me off-balance. I hit the cement, hard. My right knee throbbed as the crusted icy snow tore a hole in my panty hose. Getting myself upright, I checked my skinned and bloodied knee. I felt the same bruised-way on the inside.

As I brushed myself off, I also vowed to push aside my misery. I had to focus on the task at hand: landing this marketing job. Sore knee and all, I guided the Chevette north of town to the Interstate Loop, parked and marched into the office of Duran Architects.

Then, a little more slow and measured, I approached the perfectly postured brunette at the reception area. "Hello," I said, introducing myself and not letting the rigid glass-and-stone structure and equally rigid lady rattle me.

"I'm Mrs. Duran," she replied with the same formal tone I

heard on the phone when I made the appointment.

"It must be your husband I have a meeting with," I said, realizing she was the boss's wife.

"That's right," her regal tone announced.

I wasn't sure why The Queen seemed to be giving me the cold shoulder, but I needed her approval so I persevered with a cheery "Nice to meet you."

Just then a door swung open and out strolled a hefty man whose hair was buzzed short with a shot of gray. "Daniel Duran, but you can call me Dan. Let's meet in here," he said, motioning toward an adjacent conference room. "Have a seat. Beckman says you've got something worth seeing."

Each of us took a seat, and then The Queen entered, closed the door behind her, and remained standing, arms folded.

I launched into my pitch, focusing first on the interior designs. After I finished, Dan glanced over to his wife, and she spoke first. "Our budget on the hospital project doesn't call for interior designer's fees."

I stared at her, dazed by her declaration.

"We can't pay for your services."

As quietly as I could, I heaved a sigh, and then scrambled to make my reply professional and precise. "There's been some confusion, then. I understand that the hospital will pay for my fees."

At that news, a grin spread across Dan's face and he slapped one of his hands on the table: "Well, then, you can move ahead with the whole concept!"

The Queen's rigid mask melted away and a smile lit up her face. "Glad to have you on board. I never did like doing the whole matchy-matchy thing of picking out paint and carpet colors."

I had the job!

Immediately after the big meeting, my heart yearned to celebrate my success with Robert, but I forced myself to hold off. He had said, "I'll call you." Those three words hung in my head. If I called him at this point, after only three days, four hours and twenty-two minutes, that was not giving Robert what he said he needed.

At least that's what I thought.

But Robert didn't call.

Each day of silence was an eternity, one stacked upon the other. I staggered through each of those days in a haze of hurt. I convinced myself he would be proud of my strength in respecting his request. That way I could deny reality and believe we would reunite. The first agonizing week inched by.

I don't remember how I survived the next couple of weeks. Then, one evening I heard a loud "You-Hoo!" from deep inside the house. My landlord, Marge, was barreling her way down the side entrance. For an elderly lady, she sure had some pep. After the bounding pace came a rapid rap on my kitchen door.

"Anybody home?" Marge swung the door open and stepped into my small space. "The other day I saw you hauling an art case up the driveway and just got a bit curious. So tell me about your art portfolio; I do some pottery myself up at the college." Marge plunked herself in a metal kitchen chair and waited for answers.

A bit overwhelmed by her sudden entry, I decided it best to be polite so I settled into a seat and began to tell her about the St. Alexius project. Soon after that, I surprisingly found myself spilling my troubles about my sorrowful heartache.

"Now, now, dear," Marge said, reaching across and giving me a big hug. "Fred's been gone nine years." Her eyes turned misty, but then she regained her composure. "But if I spent time dwelling on that loss, I wouldn't be living, would I? And I've had quite the life. Most people see me as a failure since I gave up being a nun to marry Fred." The spark in her eye reassured me. "That's right, dearie. But I've experienced more love in a lifetime than most. The good Lord has supported me every step of the way. Just like going up to the college. It's not just a place to learn, but a place to embrace fellowship." She gently patted my shoulder. "I'm going there tomorrow. Meet me at my car at nine sharp, and I'll give you a tour of the art department."

She made it impossible to decline her kind offer.

In the misty morning light, all I really wanted to do was hide under the covers. Then I thought of Marge's tenacity to tackle life. Her powerful drive to grasp the moment and enjoy it to its fullest gave me the motivation to crawl to the shower.

Soon, outside Marge was waiting in her Buick. I slid onto the broad bench seat and noticed the little lady sat on a pillow to peer over the massive steering wheel and enormous hood. She turned over the engine of the big old Buick and it rumbled to life.

"Yep, 'Old Trusty' gets me where I need to go every time," Marge said, appreciatively patting the broad dashboard.

She pointed the beast away from downtown. It cornered like a bulldozer.

After we cruised a couple of miles, the flat, open prairie came into view. Minutes later, I could make out our destination as the three-story college buildings poked up like skyscrapers in the flat distance. We motored past the welcome sign for Bismarck State College and she parked in front of a brick building.

Once inside, Marge led me to the ceramic studio. Idle jugs sat on shelves and an earthy smell of wet clay filled the quiet room.

"There's no class until ten, but come this way." She guided me through a doorway.

As I stepped into the next room, I felt a distinctive vibe. Young heads bobbed to the beat of music from the Walkmans in their pocket or clipped to a waistband. They stood facing easels while painting large-scale canvases into bold statements. I felt every year their senior at the age of thirty-five.

Not Marge.

Students seemed to snap to attention when she entered the room. They gave her hand slaps and flashed ear-to-ear grins. No, age was largely irrelevant here. Marge was right; this was a fine place for friendships.

"This is Karen Jansen; she paints watercolors, too," Marge said as she placed a gentle hand on the shoulder of a brunette with loose curls. Karen stopped her paintbrush in mid-stroke and turned to me in genuine interest.

"How long have you been painting?" she asked.

"Almost four years."

She peppered me with more questions and was attentive to what I had to say about my favorite painting techniques. Like Marge, Karen drew me in.

Then Karen shared an idea with me. "I volunteer at the local art association, which I think you'd like. And it'd be an honor for us to have you teach a class there."

Her confidence in me soothed a bit of my deeply wounded pride and sense of self-worth. It made me smile from the inside out.

"Well, I've taken some great classes," I offered, thinking

of the exceptional adult education teachers I had in Michigan. "But I've never taught others."

Karen was undeterred. "Heck, you know more than we do. Plus the instructors make good money. You could even bump up your prices by teaching an advanced class, especially with the techniques you just told me about."

I felt a tiny zing of warmth and energy pierce through my loneliness.

"Nothing to be done except move forward," Marge said, noting that the conversation was doing me some good.

I let Karen's idea and Marge's comment wash over me. I liked the idea of moving forward. Securing another art position to compliment the hospital work felt like one giant step toward Robert believing my creativity could amount to a "real" job. I became certain that he would call any day.

Chapter 27

Not What I Expected

Although my name soon appeared in the newspaper as a new instructor for the Bismarck Art and Gallery Association, the phone never rang with Robert's voice saying, "Hello, I see you have another new job!"

Outside the narrow basement window, a single withered leaf sailed by, looking as fragile as I felt in my kitchen chair, arms huddled around my bent knees, blinking back tears. I drew a deep breath, telling myself: G*ive him time ... Give him time...*I had slumped through March and sagged into April enduring five weeks of despair since he asked me to get a place of my own.

At the ribbon cutting ceremony for the pediatric unit, I held my chin high in pride as everyone enjoyed my whimsical critters on the walls, adding color and personality to the sterile patient rooms. Adding a brighter punch were my selections of coordinating wallpaper boarders that pulled the entire project together.

Sadly, I had to force the smile during the event as I realized Robert was a no-show.

All alone on an important day like that was not how I had envisioned my life!

Since I was old enough to remember, I'd chased boys, always having a beau on my arm, and dreaming of marriage like Mom. When Donny, my high school sweetheart, didn't propose, I chose the quick twenty-month nursing program, preparing myself for the caretaker role for which I was destined. Then, when I achieved that role with Wayne, I made a startling discovery. Instead of the joy, I thought I'd find in marriage and family, I felt confused.

Perplexed by my uncertainties, I muddled along, eventually racing to Robert. I thought he had all my answers. Things were not working out in the blissful way I had imagined.

I found myself alone with Robert's haunting words echoing in my head: "I'll call you." It had been five weeks, and he hadn't even the decency to check in on me! Five weeks since he simply, flatly asked me to leave. Five weeks since he broke all the promises he had made to me! A sudden heat hit my face.

My thoughts simmered and I stomped in a circle in my cramped basement apartment.

The least he could do was to make sure I was okay!

Or was I that easy to forget?!

I felt the anger crushing my chest. My feet pounced harder as I paced the tight circle. The third time around, I punt-kicked the laundry basket. Clothes flew in all directions. I snatched up an armful and heaved the clothes across the room. I needed air. Yanking the door open, I marched outside. My stomping turned into a jog. I hated running, but I sprinted anyway, hard and fast. The pain of my panting lungs masked the pain in my heart, at least for a moment. Quickly I was out of breath and my chest burned like a furnace. I bent over, propping my hands on my knees, gasping for air. Then

I rose and wailed to the world, *Why me! Why me? Why me!*

My voice became hoarse, and exhaustion spread through me. I shuffled home. The phone was ringing, but I didn't have the energy to pick up the call.

A chirpy lady's voice trilled on the answering machine. "This is Satrom Travel. Your flight to Grand Rapids in two weeks has a time change. Please call us at 258-5000."

My boys. I flashed to my last visit with them from a couple of weeks earlier. I hadn't had the courage to tell anyone I had been abandoned in Bismarck. Too embarrassed to admit defeat, I pretended everything was fine.

The phone rang again. I stood too numb to move. "This is Leslie Koch, Mr. Beckman's administrative assistant at St. Alexius. Mr. Beckman requests an additional eleven pieces of the pediatric corridor art. Call me."

In my stupor I sorted out key words. Eleven corridor pieces! This was huge … not only in the size of art but in the quantity. It would complete my proposal to design all twelve calendar images of Alex and his feline friends romping in every season. *Focus,* I commanded myself. I had used my last airline voucher from Robert on my previous trip. The only way I could afford my next ticket to visit the boys was to finish the St. Alexius project.

The phone rang once more. Daze-like, I listened. "This is Paul Brandt from Duran Architects. We have another interior design project for you. Can you come by Friday at 10? Please call and confirm."

Since the success of my color scheme for the pediatric wing, the architectural firm had been using me for other projects. I felt my heart lighten a bit. When I brainstormed with the architects, I no longer felt caught in the middle. In nursing, I often felt wedged between patient rights and insurance companies dictating the duration of a patient stay. The synergy from networking with the architects eased my personal sorrow. When the professionals listened and supported my interior design ideas, it filled me with pride.

Then the phone rang one more time. A familiar voice hit me.

I picked up the phone to beat the answering machine and found just enough strength to push out a monosyllabic "Hi."

"I need to see you." There was no mistaking that deep, smooth-as-honey voice of Robert's. "Can I come by in half an hour?"

His words seemed strange, as a fog filled my head. I didn't know what to think or expect but I agreed to his request.

Shortly, when a rap came on the back apartment door, I felt my insides tremble. My pulse quickened and my breathing labored.

He stood motionless, hovering in the doorframe. His stiff posture told me he wasn't here for a casual visit. This was business. Worse yet, when I looked into his blue eyes, they were cold shards of broken sea glass, not the dreamy ones I longed for.

He thrust a file folder toward me and said, "I need your signature on these mortgage papers."

Reality slapped me awake. "You're selling the condo?"

He nodded, eyes dropping to the folder. He opened to the documents and extended a pen he had at the ready.

Officially I knew it was Robert's money tied up in the condo loan. I had been an insignificant name on the lower line ... one he had to get rid of if he was moving. I managed two words through a tightly squeezed throat. "You're leaving?"

He nodded. "I'll be gone in ten days – on May first."

Robert wasn't just taking a leave; he said, "gone." Like in vanish.

A hard and sharp stab pierced my core. "Moving where?"

"To the Carolinas."

"Why?"

"It's a great offer."

My mind spun more. Five months ago, around Christmas time, Bismarck had been the great offer. This wasn't making any sense. "Do you know someone there?"

"No, but it's warmer." He faked a shiver. I thought I saw a flash of his infectious humor, but no, nothing but another direct answer. "So I need you to sign the papers."

"You're going alone?"

He nodded as his eyes cast downward to avoid my pleading gaze.

"You're moving five states away to be alone?"

"It's a chance to start over. Bismarck isn't giving me what I need."

For six weeks I had held strong to the belief that "we" was what Robert eventually needed. Then, reality grabbed my shoulders and shook me. The horrific words of "Bismarck isn't giving me what **I** need" resonated in my ears.

Had our courtship been my imagination? The lustful feelings, his power to persuade me ... they had been so real for me. Somehow, I got the words out: "Did you ever love me?"

He kept his eyes on the floor. "I did."

Our use of the past tense crushed my heart. Hopelessness flooded me with dread and doom. The past six weeks of agonizing separation had taken all my energy just to exist. Robert's sudden slap of hurtful words hit so hard they left me too stunned to feel anything else.

"Please, just sign."

He nudged the pen into my hand. I barely had enough strength to wrap my fingers around it. All fight was gone. With a shaky hand I signed the papers.

Once my name filled the dotted line, he gathered the envelope and took a step back. Having never left the door-frame, he was back outside in one quick turn. "I'm sorry, but this is what I need. Take care." While he fled, I stood rooted in place, unable to move.

Chapter 28

College at Thirty-Plus

It replayed in my mind over and over, Robert's quest to escape from me, from Bismarck, from the Midwest. As the days crept by, I had wanted to call him one more time, but I wasn't strong enough to hear the same words: "This isn't about you, it's about me."

The endless days trailed on, and I wobbled back into denial – the first stage of grieving – but I couldn't cling to that in reality. The first of May had crawled by a few weeks ago and Robert was gone. No denying that.

Then I forged my way up to anger – stage two for grieving – shouting *I trusted you!* I stomped and screamed for countless days. Or was it weeks?

Bargaining, the third stage of grieving, didn't work so well as a coping mechanism because he was 1,744 miles away by then.

The drawn-out days dragged on as I wilted into the woefulness of the fourth stage – depression. This cloak of sadness took all my energy as I floundered through the month of June.

Yes, I could flee back to Michigan, but I felt used and stupid and hurt all at the same time. Shame kept me from wanting to show my face to all the people who'd gawked at me and shook their heads at my decision to leave Wayne. Especially Mom.

I was too weak to move back to face her straightforward-ness. She had a way of scolding me with that raised eyebrow and silence. If I went back to Michigan at that point, her words of "I told you so" would crush me. I could barely admit to myself what a foolish mistake I had made.

My embarrassment magnified when I reflected on the fact that I had only been in Bismarck for six months. Worse yet, just three months since that first night when I saw no promise ring on Robert.

The chock-hold of grieving surrounded me. I flopped facedown onto my bed, utterly deflated. Once again I had no one to blame but myself. I was the culprit, not the victim. From making bad choices, I created quite a mess. I ran from the loneliness of my marriage and life at the Colonial into Robert's arms. *Was I being punished for being so reckless?* I had pushed away my sons only to have Robert push me away.

My boys. My heart yearned for them. I knew I had to pull myself together because it was Wednesday, one of my let-ter-writing days to the boys. I picked up a pencil and began writing a short story to them, letting my mind drift to one of our fond memories. Since the day Wayne and I separated, I faithfully wrote or drew a cartoon to the boys every Monday, Wednesday, and Friday and I called every Sunday.

Pulling out a twenty-five cent postage stamp, even though the recent three-cent price hike strained my meager budget, I licked it and stuck it to the addressed envelope. I always felt a bit lighter after "talking" to my sons this way.

As for the Sunday phone calls, lately my mother-hen

instincts had been on full alert. Wayne had plans to remarry.

I listened with scrutiny for a hint of conflict or words of upset from the boys. Instead they giggled about other news: a new guinea pig! However, that wasn't enough to satisfy my curiosity. Luckily I had a friend, Denise Hoffman, from my earlier days in Michigan who had reached out to me. When I heard there was a woman in Wayne's life, meaning my boys' life, I dialed up Denise.

She gave me a full report, saying the new woman, a teacher, matched Wayne's need for routines. I also knew being a single parent could be a struggle. Therefore, if Wayne's life was easier and happier, then the boys' lives would be, too.

I kept those thoughts in the forefront and shoved aside any visions of the boys' day-to-day life with someone besides Wayne. *Don't go there,* I coached myself.

In my dinky apartment, I dragged myself from the bed and scuffed past the tiny kitchen table. Propped against the wall was one of the remaining eleven corridor art pieces I had to install at St. Alexius. This art freelance job offered me a flexible schedule and paid me well enough to return monthly to visit the boys.

I had been fortunate to have the Bismarck community provide me with an opportunity to grow in the arts. The comfort from this North Dakota city made the choice to finish the St. Alexius project easier, especially compared to the humiliation that surely awaited me back in Michigan.

Focusing on Alex the Cat reminded me with gratitude that my current livelihood in the arts was coming directly from the Bismarck community. I had schmoozed my way with Mr. Snider, dean of the hospital, but I clearly lacked the credentials to sell my marketing skills to a hospital anywhere else.

I heard Marge's Buick rumble to life, and from the narrow window, I saw the huge hubcaps roll away. She was heading to the college.

Then an idea began to take shape. If I added college classes to my self-taught marketing ideas, they would enrich my business knowledge and boost my credibility to obtain future marketing jobs beyond just Bismarck. I could move closer to my sons and stay in the field of art. I felt a small wedge of lightness inside ... something I hadn't felt since Robert asked me to move out of the condo three months ago.

Remembering a newspaper headline I had read while waiting in the grocery line gave me another idea. Bismarck Hospital, the across-the-street competitor to St. Alexius, was renaming itself MedCenter One. This was a groundbreaking development, historically speaking, because hospitals paid little attention to marketing in the past. Hospital administration had been all about patient care instead.

I had spent thirteen years in six different hospitals, some large, some small, and could see that the delivery of medical services was becoming much more competitive. The rebranding of MedCenter One confirmed that, and it meant my marketing ideas could also be on target in Michigan. Gaining education in the field seemed like the perfect next step for me to return home and work in an artistic field.

On the scary side, though, it had been fourteen years since I had attended a college class. *Could I compete with those eager young minds with boundless energy? And what about the cost?* I took a deep breath and pushed down my insecurities. I was getting better at compartmentalizing.

I thumbed through the phone book, readying myself: *Be brave ... do it for the boys ... make them proud. After all, self-improvement was a lesson I wanted to teach them. What better way than to be my own example!*

I found the local college that Marge attended, took a deep breath, and dialed.

Admissions said they had an opening for that afternoon. Afraid that if I didn't say yes, I might change my mind, I accepted the appointment.

By dinnertime ... it was official. The next week I would be starting a four-week July semester as a full-time student taking basic business classes in pursuit of a marketing degree. The bubbly blonde in Admissions had made it sound so easy. "Time-wise, you're considered a resident of North Dakota, which saves money."

A resident of North Dakota. Eight months ago when Robert mentioned relocating, all I knew about this state was that it was somewhere south of Canada. *How had I dug such a deep hole of shame in such a short time?*

Then another ray of hope emerged. "Make sure you apply for some scholarships," the blonde's bright tone continued. "The full-ride ones are all taken, but if you root through these reference books, we find there are always small sums waiting to be taken." She pulled out a desk chair and left me to "apply" myself.

The scholarship forms were easy, and if I snagged enough of them, they could almost pay my entire bill. I just had to be studious enough to fill out seven different ten-page, triple-copy forms. By the end of the afternoon, with a pinched hand, I was one step closer to a college life I could afford.

Before I left, the blonde barreled into the room waving my new class schedule. "Did you also know that for anything above fifteen credits of enrollment the tuition is a flat fee? No extra charge. Is there maybe another class you'd like to try?"

My mind raced through the accounting and economics class on my schedule. Important classes, yes, but endless columns of numbers were not going to suit my passion to color outside of the lines. On a whim, I enrolled in my first art elective.

Who knew it would change my world.

I started at square one with Basic Drawing 101.

In an early class exercise, I scribbled contour lines in an out-of-control pattern as I moved the pencil across a blank piece of drawing paper. I felt like I was back in kindergarten, despite pounding on the door of thirty-five. I pushed aside my insecurities, remembering that at the onset of class the professor explained, "Contour drawing is the backbone for improving hand-eye coordination, which is the fundamental necessity of an artist."

Next were the laborious detail exercises of establishing the vanishing points in perspective. Flashbacks of frustration at art camp when I was fifteen raced through my mind. Fortunately, this time, I had more respect for learning the basic mechanics of art to achieve a quality result.

In short order, I learned that this instructor would no longer let me get away with the flimsy watercolor techniques of my past. Once, while applying shading to a charcoal drawing, he pointed a finger at the photograph I used as a reference. "Look closely at the positive and negative shapes. Study the texture and pattern. Mimic those." Then he pondered my sketch a bit more. "Hmm. You might consider starting over."

"Starting over?" I grumbled under my breath. *I've been trying to start over for four painful months since Robert asked me to leave the condo.*

However, if I wanted to grow, constructive criticism was an important component of how I would get there. I bit my lip, listened to his advice, and started over. Talk about an eye-opening moment for me! The new piece radiated with freshness and captured some realistic movement. Clearly, basic drawing skills were the mainstay of good art.

Soon, though, I had another major lesson to learn.

Chapter 29
A Goal of My Own

Stumbling through July, I rode the emotional waves as they hit me. For the first time in more than five months since I had moved into my apartment, it seemed their intensity had lessened. That sack-of-sorrow I'd been carrying around felt a bit lighter. Then a single comment I overheard changed my life.

After having turned in the final sketches for preschool and elementary kids' coloring books, I strolled down the corridor of St. Alexius with pride. Alex the Cat would not only be on the walls of the pediatric unit, he would be hitting the printing presses.

I wedged myself in an elevator among two nurses. They huddled in front of me and their whispered voices echoed in the small chamber. "I heard that Curtis, our private college theater director, finished the semester and immediately moved to North Carolina to live with Dr. R!"

As I stood behind them, my mind started spinning faster than the pulley running our elevator. *Someone had joined Robert? To live with him? He'd told me he was moving alone. And if what they said was true, apparently he had been involved with this man all along?!*

The elevator stopped, the bell dinged, I got off, and rushed out the front door. Outside the air was cooler; I pulled it into my lungs in giant gasps. As my heart rate slowed, I began to take in calmer, longer breaths.

Alone with my thoughts, I heard Robert's request circle around me: *"I need time to think."* I assumed he had been thinking about "us." I reflected on the nurse's comment. More clues from Robert's previous words hit me. *"Embrace yourself. You be you, not what others want or expect."* Suddenly, pieces clicked in my mind. I had never dreamed of him having his own inner struggles.

Then the truth finally struck me. Robert's decision to leave Bismarck wasn't about me. Or about my art. Or any flaw or ineptitude on my part. This was about Robert. This was something I couldn't control.

For five months, self-doubt about what I had done wrong for Robert to want us to separate had devastated my confidence and pride. But right then, standing outside in the comfort of a cool July morning, I realized this was not about me! If he loved a man, there was nothing I could have ever done to make him happy.

As quickly as that sense of relief hit me, self-doubt reared its ugly head once again. *Did I miss vital clues along the way?* As my mind traced over my time with Robert, I began to see signs in retrospect that I had been blind to before. *Did it go back as far as trying new things like the Spanish lessons? His every Wednesday night of privacy? What about Scott, the Michigan condo neighbor who was "visiting" when I was in Michigan? Or what about Robert having me drive myself to the airport because he wanted to explore beyond Bismarck when I was out of town?*

Looking back, the clues seemed to be there, yet strewn so far apart and wedged between romantic gifts and promises he had made to me. No wonder I didn't catch them ... but why didn't he handle things better? *Why did he lead me on and bring me all the way out here?*

Anger rose hot and replaced self-doubt. I felt deceived! *How could he have lied to me for so long? Worse, he let me move a thousand miles away from my sons!* My chest felt like a fireball as I let out a fierce wail that turned into soggy sobs by the time I shuffled to the parking lot. I yanked open the door of the car, sunk inside, and pounded my fists on the steering wheel. More sobs escaped. I don't remember how long I languished there. I came to my senses with a dull ache in my head. Then still more of Robert's words rushed back: "I feel freer out here." *Did it take moving to North Dakota for him to stop fooling himself?*

So many questions, but at least I could see many of them were Robert's issues. Except for one: Where did all this leave me?

The next few days I slowly felt myself let go of the pain ... the drama. More days passed. I don't remember how many because I was drowning in humiliation. I could accept my naivety in missing the signs of Robert's infidelity, but shamefully I had to admit it was my decision to move a thousand miles on a promise. Robert had never twisted my arm. I let his tender touch tantalize me, thinking he could make me happy.

Memories of my past ran through my mind. As a tween, I chased after my older brother's friends, looking from one boy to the next to make me giggle, make me feel important, and to make me whole. In fact, I had been doing it not just during my childhood, but my teenage, and college days, too.

I came to understand I had developed a pattern: I had always been looking for someone to take care of me and complete me. I had a "follower's" addiction – if there even was such a thing. I decided it didn't matter if my addiction had a name; the dependency was as powerful as alcohol or drugs. Moreover, it had plagued me.

For all those years, I never once thought to look inside myself and consider not depending on someone else for my happiness.

Standing in the darkened kitchen of night with the tile floor cool on my feet, the reality of my weakness sent a shiver through me. If I didn't break this behavior I had been repeating time and again, I would never like who I was.

A sliver of the cloud-covered moon broke through the narrow window of the apartment, lighting up photographs of the boys in soccer uniforms that were clipped to the refrigerator. Their mile-wide smiles filled my soul, and I yearned to be closer.

I realized life was still going on, with or without me. It was up to me to decide what part I would play in it. I could be the quitting kind ... or not. If I expected resilience from my sons, I needed to expect it from myself. *Could I be brave enough to go after an art career?*

When I discovered watercolor back when I was with Wayne, I considered art as simply a hobby. With Robert, I sought part-time art jobs, thinking I could mix my painting in between doting on him. Then when I returned to college, my confidence rallied around a business degree in marketing. Yet that one art elective, Basic Drawing 101, was what really pushed me. This was such a strange and good feeling, to focus on a career that could bring me challenges and joy. *How far could I go? What significance might I make in the world?* Anything could happen and I wanted to find out.

It felt good to be pushing toward a goal of my own ... *A goal of my own. Had I ever had one of those?*

Chapter 30
Pushing Forward

The sight of the late July hydrangea bush was a bold visual statement in my neighbors' yard. The beauty made my head turn. A year earlier, Robert had plucked that same snowball-shaped flower for me as an ardent gift after my first art fair. Surprisingly, I noticed my heart barely beat faster. At that moment I realized I had survived the worst of Robert's rejection. Once he moved to the Carolinas, almost three months ago, I never heard from him again. Oddly, I never ran into his family when I visited Michigan, either. I suppose that was a good thing. I don't know what I would have said to them.

As I looked a little longer at the hydrangea, I noticed one of the blooms had a tint of blue – the same hue as my aquamarine ring from Robert. Once again I surprised myself when I reflected on the ring. Like the hydrangea, it held memories, yet I discovered my mind moved forward. *Why not pawn that ring for my next plane ticket to see the boys? Yes! I could do that!* My heart felt stronger focused on the boys instead of attached to a romantic trinket.

The ring brought decent money, enough for a ticket and enough to take the next step toward fulfilling my moving-back-home goal. To establish business contacts beyond Bismarck, I needed top-quality photographs of my watercolors so I could enter elite art fairs, shows and competitions. Unfortunately, the only thing I knew about photographing artwork was how to take the pictures outdoors for the best light and least amount of glare. However, gusty wind and bird droppings never gave me good results.

Duran Architects recommended a commercial photographer named Larry Weller, so I tracked him down in Bismarck. Soon I was visiting his office, standing in a quiet reception area. A door opened, and a man with raven-black hair and mustache filled the doorway. His more than six-foot frame made me think the hefty truck I had parked alongside could be his because this guy would never squeeze into a pint-size Chevette.

"Hey there, I'm Larry Weller," he said as he shot off a carefree smile. "Dan told me you needed some presentation photos."

"I do." Instantly I liked his straight-down-to-business approach. Because his hourly fees were a luxury, working efficiently suited me just fine.

Right away he worked with energy, yet with a natural ease that seemed as casual as his open collared knit shirt. The bill was reasonable so I only had to eat macaroni for a week.

Back at the apartment, I threw out my blurry, bird-anointed photographs. Having quality professional slides felt like a small victory. I just had to beat my competitors for a spot in the coveted Minneapolis Uptown Art Fair and a few other shows I was hoping to schedule for income.

While I chipped away at my college classes, my drawing instructor had assigned me a desk in the art department.

Better yet, I could work there anytime! This off-in-the-corner desk allowed me to absorb other lessons. Daily I spent long hours listening, learning ... and improving!

The many hours I put in at that desk also eased the isolation of the basement apartment. I would leave before dawn and not return until late evening. Still, crawling into bed alone each night was the emptiest feeling of all. In the darkness, when things calmed down and grew still, I would feel the pain of loneliness clutch around me.

To erase the emptiness and help me fall asleep, I punched the play button on a mini tape recorder and listened to Mozart's Clarinet Concerto. Often, haunting dreams woke me, always with an image of the boys' hands reaching out; then again I would hit the button and wait for the classical music to settle my nerves. Some nights I had to tap that button many times.

Chapter 31
Rain on My Parade

The last day of July dawned hot. Even in the early morning, heat waves shimmered above the asphalt as I headed toward Rapid City, South Dakota, for the first art fair of the season. I leaned forward and my shirt peeled away from the vinyl fabric of the non-air conditioned Chevette.

An hour later I rolled across the South Dakota border. The flat, barren terrain behind me yielded to the foothills of the Black Hills. Going up the long inclines, the Chevette lost oomph, dropping quickly from 55 to 50 to 45 miles per hour. I punched the clutch and downshifted the manual four-cylinder into third gear. I spotted a puff of smoke from the exhaust.

With the little compact brimming full of watercolor paintings on which I had labored many late nights, I hoped for some decent income at the art fair, but not for an auto repair. I had shaken the last nickels out of my coin jar to pay the local glass and art supply store for metal frames, mat boards, and glass.

As the Chevette struggled up another hill, I saw no further signs of smoke, so I chalked it up to aggressive downshifting on the previous incline.

Crisis averted, I felt a pleasant snap of brightness inside.

Something told me to push, to keep trying; there was something better out there even though recent times had been as bumpy as this rural road, SD 79.

As I crested the top of another massive hill on the national forest Black Hills border, a dark and brooding western sky appeared. Then a gust of wind soared and shook the Chevette. A hot morning rain began to ping the thin metal roof, smacking the car like sodden spitballs. I clicked the wipers to full-speed, but the windshield stayed a slick blur.

Finally, as I plowed in to the town of Spearfish, the sun peeked out. The roads were still wet as I pumped the squeaky brakes and slowed to a stop. It was the first stoplight I'd approached for more than a hundred miles.

When I brought the Chevette to a halt, a wave of water from the back seat sloshed onto my feet. Instantly, my heels were swimming in a pool. I eased the Chevette to the shoulder of the road and parked. *Where had all the water come from?*

Needing to explore, I bailed out of the Chevette and gazed under the driver's side wheel well, discovering a hole the size of a cannonball.

From behind I heard a rough voice. "Got some car trouble there?"

Startled, I jumped and turned toward the man's voice.

"The engine giving you a problem, or something else?"

The man's head was capped with white hair and then crowned with a gray cowboy hat. The brim shaded his dark eyes, and his face had a wrinkle for every year he'd been around, maybe seventy.

After casting my eyes toward the lagoon in the Chevette floorboards, I looked up to see the man peer wide-eyed at the interior pond.

"That storm was a real downpour. I've never seen the likes of that."

I peeled back the rubber floor mat. In one area, daylight shone all the way from the front bumper.

"That hole would have sunk the Titanic," he said. "Darn road salt ate your metal." He bent for a closer look. "I'm surprised your whole foot didn't punch through."

I shifted my feet and my water-logged shoes squished. "I was dry while driving," I said. "But when I slowed to a stop ..."

"...all the water rushed forward!" He took the words right out of my mouth. "Your momentum held it all in place until you stopped. I can drill a hole in your floorboard to let out that water. I have the right drill in the truck. I'll get my tools."

Straightaway he returned, swinging a toolbox and a piece of sheet metal. "My son and I own a heating and cooling business. Just your lucky day."

Lucky? I'd driven a hundred miles at turtle speed in a downpour to find myself hung up on the side of the road with another soon-to-be hole drilled in a rust-bucket of a car. At this rate I would miss the art fair set-up and lose my chance for much-needed cash.

No. I didn't feel lucky at the moment.

However, I did feel the kindness of strangers.

My friendly helper wormed himself under the Chevette, and soon I heard the whirr of a power drill. A small stream of water drained onto the ground. He wriggled his way out, rose, exchanged the drill for a huge, paper-punch gadget and then crawled inside the driver's side, wedging himself under the steering wheel. He placed his sheet of metal over the bowling ball-size hole and shot button-like snaps from the gun to anchor the metal patch.

Viola. A decent little floorboard made out of ductwork.

"How can I ever thank you?" I asked the handy stranger with no name. "What do I owe you?"

He waved me off. "Aww. Glad I could help. I have a daughter about your age, and I hope if she needed a helping hand someone would offer up a bit of decency." He tipped his hat my way and headed off to his truck.

I gazed at the now-cloudless bright blue sky and said silent thanks for the lift in the weather, the stranger who riveted my car, and the many kindred spirits I'd encountered in the Dakotas: Mr. Stahl, Mark the Mechanic, Marge, the landlady. The people of North Dakota were helping to rebuild me, one kindness at a time.

A car whooshed by, snapping me back to reality. I checked my watch. There was still time to make it to Rapid City!

By 10 a.m. I had finished my set-up, and a breeze-free scorcher was upon us at the art fair. As the crowds circulated, I hid under a canopy of beech trees but the heat still roasted me. Then the judging panel came by, in the midst of a steady flow of customers, and handed me an official-looking prize.

"You got Best of Show!" howled my neighbor, a sculptor, as he clapped me on the back. "That's quite an honor!"

I felt elated. My first ribbon ... and it was blue, no less! I had won!

Even more satisfying, I received an invitation from the prestigious Dahl Art Center to display future work. I tried to wipe away the ridiculous grin that spread across my face and act professional. I had my first contact for future work and income outside of Bismarck!

It may have taken me five months of living alone in Bismarck to achieve this first step to be able to move back to

Michigan with national art contacts in hand, but it was a prideful step. If I could land a few more contacts outside of Bismarck, I could move home feeling more accomplished. I'd be earning a living in my field. It would go a long way toward healing my self-confidence.

I thought of my upcoming long visit with the boys. That would be the best celebration for me.

Even if it was six weeks of camping, with bug spray as my only perfume, I knew I'd enjoy every second of it.

* * *

For more than a month, the boys and I had been living in a hot tin box, my dad's travel trailer, during our big summer break together. For my sons at least, a daily camping uniform of flip-flops informality was a dream-come-true. Brian was nine and Adam was eight. In their camp life together, Adam seemed to initiate most of the mischief. Recently he tried to hog-tie Brian with red licorice ropes to keep his brother from getting first dibs on the morning doughnuts.

Nearing the end of the vacation, Brian dragged his bare feet though the sand and then plopped down onto our picnic table. I sat next to him and waited. It usually took a spell for this logical thinker to share his thoughts.

Under the table he was drawing circles in the sand with his big toe. "My stomach feels funny." Right off I noticed his watery eyes. He was gazing downward, at the Detroit Tigers ball-cap he was spinning in his hands.

I placed my hand on his forehead. "You don't feel like you have a fever. Let's take a walk to the camp store to look for something to settle an upset stomach."

My fact-loving kid appreciated something tangible with which to label his feelings while the hard truth gnawed at our guts. We would be saying good-bye in a few days, and that was never easy.

Brian nibbled on his lower lip as we strolled toward the store. "Camping is more fun than living with Dad," he said.

I looped an arm around his shoulder and gave a squeeze. "Of course, it is. There's no school." I tried to make light of his comment to keep the conversation going. Brian was quick to stay quiet instead of exploring his feelings.

"But it's different at Dad's," he added.

I gave his shoulder a squeeze. "And my house would be different than camping if you lived your school year with me. Can you picture me asking about your homework?" I stopped walking and acted out the everyday-parent role by narrowing my eyebrows into a stern, expectant look.

He blinked back emotions, chewing his lip. "But, Mom."

My stomach twisted and I felt my own eyes fill. I had to hold it together to help my son. I squatted down next to him and met his green eyes.

"Is this about more changes than just a new guinea pig joining your family? What does it feel like inside here about your dad getting married?" I tapped his chest where his heart beat fast.

"Oh, there's not much to that. We do everything together now. Things will be about the same with Dad getting married."

"Hmm." I let some time drift between us.

Brian stayed silent, not giving me anything more.

I plopped down into the sand and he sat alongside me. *How can I help my son?* I made a big sweep of the campground. "Fishing and frog catching are a lot better than school. But there is another reason this is so different from your dad's house. Rules need to be tougher to get to school on time. We don't have rules on vacation. I'm sure that makes it hard for you."

He gave a quiet nod.

I pressed on. "The important thing is you remember your dad loves you as much as I do, and that's what matters the most. We will always be there for you, just in different ways."

His lower lip still hung low.

"We've talked about how a consistent schedule makes your life easier. It helps you stay focused on what's important – and that's you!" I placed my hand over his heart. "You are so special."

His lip pulled in and one corner of his mouth tilted up. I took it as a good sign.

"Then let's see what we can find at the camp store. Maybe some cherry-flavored ChapStick for those lips."

"Watermelon would be better." He plopped his cap back on his head.

Chapter 32
Odd Jobs

On a crisp day in October, I opened my apartment door to find a dead bird lying at my doormat. Eight months earlier, when I found myself unexpectedly living alone, I felt like that fragile bird with its life whisked out of him. Thankfully I was learning to fly on my own.

The bark of a dog pulled me out of my trance. Annie, the springer spaniel puppy from next door, spun in a circle, plopped her furry butt down, and yipped again.

Over the past months, this dog had wormed her way beneath my skin and curled around my heart, easing my loneliness. One nuzzle from Annie and a smile would bubble up and burst across my face. It felt so good to laugh – all because of a dog.

"Why on Earth did you plant that dead bird here?" Then I remembered. A short time earlier, a friend had dropped off a dozen bronze and black pheasant feathers for an art collage. The delivery must have kicked in the puppy's retrieving instincts.

Although the bird corpse was a trophy Annie presented to me, I scooped it up and buried it in the backyard. All the while Annie looked on with eyes the color of smooth rum.

That rich amber color reminded me that, on some nights when the loneliness sliced through me, I had tried alcohol to mask my sorrows and ease me to sleep. I learned the opposite was the case for me: Drinking didn't hide anything. The emptiness still tracked me down when I woke up. Instead, I found one look from Annie was more intoxicating than whiskey. Her yips brightened my day and her face licks made me giggle.

Unable to resist the incredible huggable pup, I whisked her into my arms. "Would you like to assist me in an unusual job?"

I needed to be on security detail at the Bismarck Art and Gallery Association during its upcoming grand exhibit in the Elan Gallery. The nonprofit didn't have surveillance cameras, so the organization needed someone to sleep in the 1907 two-story home for insurance purposes. I volunteered and, in return, Elan Executive Director Greta Johansson scheduled a private exhibit of my work and waived the 50 percent commission fee normally assessed on all sales.

A show at the prestigious Elan would be a feather in my cap, and with no commission, I was tail-wagging like Annie.

The pup's owners, the Grunners, agreed to let Annie go overnight with me. While Annie rode the six blocks to the gallery in excitement, I had trepidations. I had negotiated over the phone with Greta, so I hadn't officially met her yet. I had only heard her reputation: small and mighty.

At the front entrance I turned the ornate doorknob of the Elan Gallery. "Hello. Hello." My voice echoed off the polished wood floors and high ceiling of the former living room, now used as an exquisite main gallery. I stared at the fine art all around.

A petite, fair-skinned blonde headed toward us from the back of the house. "I'm Greta Johansson." She had a cool edge to her voice and was dressed in heels and a tailored suit that were as crisp as her words. She didn't give a blink to Annie. "I just finished setting up the cot in the privacy of the office."

Following the peck of her heels, we scurried behind and entered a small kitchen. From behind the back door, we heard a bark. Instantly Annie tugged at her leash.

"Uh, that's Snowball." Greta's face flushed as she opened the door to a little white marshmallow of a mutt.

"The Elan is a professional place of business," she said, planting her hands firmly on her hips while addressing the pooch more than us. "So during operating hours, Snowball stays outside." Then she softened a bit. "Since the gallery is officially closed now, I suppose we can let these two visit while I review with you the rest of your responsibilities." While Annie pranced about, Snowball's tail wagged so his entire back end shimmied.

After thorough instructions, Greta and Snowball left and I secured the locks.

Back in the office area I noticed a copy of Fanfare magazine posted on the corkboard above Greta's desk. The monthly publication featured entrepreneurs and prominent business leaders in the Bismarck community. I was looking at my face plastered on the front of the magazine.

It was an article about me!

More than a month earlier, Fanfare had interviewed me. What an honor! However, I never dreamed important people, like Greta, would save it! Next I noticed a yellow sticky note attached. It said: *Kate Moynihan's show is coming here!* Greta's business success humbled me. I never imagined that

*Me on the cover of the prominent
Bismarck business publication*

she saw something in me! My ever-present self-doubt was
hard at work again.

Uneventful hours passed. Under the cot Annie had curled
up and started to snore so I crawled onto the army-stiff wool
coverlet and found it impossible to get comfortable there.
I wondered if this harebrained idea of house sitting was
worth the effort, but the thought of a show at Elan eventually
soothed me to sleep.

In a half-awake haze, I periodically heard muffled barks from outside.

Then, a little after two o'clock, Annie yapped, indicating she wanted to go outside to do her business. When I opened the door, Snowball scooted in! My sleepy thoughts began to coalesce. "You were that bark I heard during the night! How long have you been ..." I gasped, certain Greta wouldn't normally let Snowball roam the streets. "Greta must be worried sick about you!"

I had to call Greta. The clock glowed 2:30 a.m. Did I risk disturbing the mighty CEO of Bismarck arts in the middle of the night? *I could lose my commission. I could lose my show.*

I paced the room. It was 2:37 a.m. The lovable pups frolicked. "I'm glad you're having a good time." Then I put myself in Greta's shoes, and decided if my dog was missing I would be worried sick. My fingers clenched the phone, and I dialed.

Greta answered on the first ring. Living quite nearby, she was at the back door only minutes later.

"Snowball never runs off!" she said, frantically waving a flashlight against the night. "I've been searching since we left!" Greta was still dressed in her business suit with her heels scuffed and soaked from racing through the dewy grass.

It turned out the small and mighty executive director of the Elan Gallery ended up hosting a big and mighty show for me. Moreover, I didn't have to spend another night on that miserable cot.

Chapter 33

Big Trouble = Big Results

Exactly forty and one eighth of an inch was the maximum cargo width of the Chevette hatchback, and I used every fraction to squeeze in the largest-size canvas I could paint to deliver a special order to Minot, North Dakota, a city an hour and half due north. To save time and money, after I delivered the commissioned art, I would set up at the Big-One, the largest art and craft show in the state.

This show was on the cusp of Christmas, so I had created some framed tabletop Christmas collages I called Paper-Shapes. As customers arrived, they swept up ten to twenty dollar jars of Hunters Choice Marinade and hand-sewn baby bibs from my nearby vendor's booths. Unfortunately, the price of one of my PaperShapes required twice that. After sitting in my booth from nine to nine the first day and until five the second, I hadn't sold a single PaperShape or painting, just a handful of handmade Christmas cards.

Later, each heavy load I hauled back to the Chevette weighed down my spirits. The hatchback was brimmed to capacity with my unsold stock, and I was blinking fast, trying to hold back tears of failure. I was counting on cash from this show.

While I was hunched over the last load, the plump older lady who ran a whimsical puppet booth strolled up to me. "Hello, dear. My name is Marva ... but you probably heard everyone call me Grammy." Her eyes sparkled as she continued, "I'm wondering if you'd trade me puppets for a small painting."

Upon hearing those words, I was certain Marva was short for Marvelous!

"Certainly!" My sons would be the envy of all their friends with the huge, creative puppets that Grammy made and sold.

With the Chevette fully packed and my confidence bolstered a bit from the puppet trade, I climbed into the driver's seat. Unfortunately, a mile later the *check engine* light flashed red against the black sky, the black plains, the black road. *Why now?* I coaxed the car to the closest service station.

When I pulled up, a young man barely sprouting facial hair and noisily chewing gum was leaning against the station door. I crawled out of the compact and shared my woes.

He lifted the hood and poked his nose deep inside. "I'm afraid it needs a complete valve job. That means rebuilding the entire engine." The gum snapped and found a parking spot in his left cheek. "Where are you headed?"

"Back to Bismarck. Tonight." I tried to make my voice sound steady, not wrought with worry; I couldn't afford a hotel room.

"What about all that stuff in the back? Can you dump it?"

Did he say dump it? "No," I croaked. "It's my livelihood."

"Sheesh!" He spit and his gum flew out. "Okay, here's

what we'll do. I'll tow you to the bus station and you can send the big stuff back to Bismarck. Without the extra weight you'll probably be able to make it the 95 miles to Bismarck without damaging the engine."

It was after six on a Sunday evening and no shipping companies worked on weekends. The bus became my only option.

"Buy a bus ticket and check this stuff as luggage. That way, if you're lucky, they'll waive the twenty-pound weight restriction and maximum fifty-dollar insurance that applies to shipping cargo."

I gasped. My art weighed more and was worth more than the cargo limits!

It turned out I bought the ticket and they accepted the boxes as luggage, all for less than a tank of gas. Then, in the empty Chevette, I coaxed the hatchback to Bismarck.

Back in my tiny apartment, I waded around the mound of unsold Christmas PaperShapes. From the bust at the Big-One, my holiday spirit sagged so low I could trip over it. I shuffled to the miniscule kitchen for a cup of coffee. From one of the three cupboards, I tugged out a mug and filled it halfway with the bitter brew.

Since moving to Bismarck nearly a year ago, I had been tackling every art lead that came my way, trying to see if I could make it in the creative world. I would rather fail at something than regret never trying. In my reading and study about business, leaders viewed failure as lessons learned. I felt every painful lesson from the tough trip to the Big-One and back.

Don't despair! I told myself. *Focus on work, not worry. Concentrate on the next task.* I needed to restack all those

PaperShapes to condense space. Tidying up the inventory took more muscle than brainpower. Quickly I found my mind wandering ... and then I struck a thought: I could sell PaperShapes to other businesses instead of trying to direct sell, like at the fairs.

I had learned creativity struck randomly for me so I jumped on the idea, punching the costs to creating each PaperShape into an adding machine. Selling PaperShapes to other businesses meant they needed a discount off retail so they would profit on each sale. I was entering the world of wholesaling. I tore off the whirling tape and calculated that I could, indeed, eek out a small profit on each piece. *Some money was better than no money.* I dialed my first contact, the Dahl Fine Art Center in Rapid City.

"Yes, ship them right out," the director said after I explained what I had in mind. "There is plenty of time to sell them for the holiday season."

Next I dialed Bruce Card's House of Gifts, the owner below Robin Gallery, in Michigan, knowing he changed his entire shop into a Christmas world.

"Sure. Send them!" he told me.

Another yes!

Packing each box of six, my sprits rose. It felt good to be taking action; it meant I had a possibility to generate income. If I took no action ... I was guaranteed nothing.

As I returned from shipping PaperShapes, from the doorway I heard the phone ringing in the apartment. Lately, all the calls were good news regarding the Christmas collages. Maybe my Karma was turning positive, I thought while running to grab the ringing phone.

"This is Mr. Carlsson. Dave Carlsson," a crusty voice barked.

"Yes." On my desk nearby, I could see the business owner's foil-embossed company card. He was the administrator of the number-one employer in Sioux Falls, South Dakota.

"We met at the Big-One craft fair this past weekend," he said ... and I remembered.

I pictured Mr. Carlsson in his itchy-looking herringbone jacket. His crisp white shirt and chokehold necktie appeared formal compared with most of the crowd of appliquéd-sweatshirt craft lovers who strolled the fair.

"I'm interested in the tree-shaped Christmas card." He referred to the handcrafted card I made individually. "But I see it's blank inside. Could you add a verse?"

"Sure." I thought I could easily scratch Happy Holidays with a metallic gold pen.

"I'd like to use my own words. A special message to my management team, perhaps a poem of about fifty words."

I gulped. Fifty words in fancy calligraphy would take time, and I'd have to practice the curvy script, yet I could ask for more money. Then I realized I had never learned the art of negotiation. Nursing taught me how to follow doctors' orders and maintain hospital protocol. I fell silent.

Before I could gather my thoughts, I heard, "Give me a quote for 215 handmade cards." He clicked off the line.

The next day a heavy mist hung outside the apartment window as I gave myself a pep talk before calling Mr. Carlsson. *The project will take more time, and you're worth it. Ask for it!*

His secretary answered and a moment later Mr. Carlsson's abrupt voice came on the line.

I turned away from the foggy window and my eyes caught the collection of the boys' photographs clipped to the refrigerator. With a newfound confidence, I laid out the fees and confirmed the deadline.

"I accept your proposal. The verse and deposit will be in the mail." And with that he hung up.

One day that week, while elbow-deep in green paint, the check arrived. I boogied to the bank waving it high in the air. Pumped with energy, I shipped the order in ten days, which was four days ahead of deadline.

Pleased with myself, I flaunted an example of the glitzy card to a college classmate.

"I know a California art manufacturing company that is requesting miniature art samples to sell to national chain stores," she said. "I'm sending an idea, and I think you should design something like this card, but with an all-occasion, everyday-décor look. The company's called International Art Concepts."

That's all it took. Through one friend's helpful comment, this simple tree collage might lead to something HUGE!

Chapter 34

A Cottage Industry is Born

I waited ... and waited some more.

It had been two weeks since I sent the tree collage sample to International Art Concepts in anticipation of landing an account to produce mini collages. There was potential for sizable orders – larger than the 215 Christmas cards for Dave Carlsson – because International Art sold to Pier One and Spiegel Catalog! *Could this be the account that would let me move back to Michigan and live off the arts?*

A trip to see the boys helped pass some more waiting time. This was to be my third visit to Michigan since Wayne remarried in late summer. That was also when he and the boys moved thirty minutes from the Colonial to another lakeshore community, Grand Haven. For the boys, new neighborhood friends became their school and sports friends. For me, I found the fresh eyes of the new city comforting, as I didn't run into the same old people with the ugly stares from back when.

As I had on previous visits, for the weekend we loaded up and drove the three hours to my parents' house in Detroit. As we approached, misery loomed large. I had decided to face Mom about what I'd been hiding for almost nine months: that I was living alone. Although I had successfully concealed the truth, I couldn't risk her not finding out much longer.

Once I voiced the first words of explanation to Mom, she hit me hard with, "I thought you said you could trust him."

Instantly humiliation filled me. Shame washed over me. Embarrassment. Inadequacy.

Before I could respond, Mom continued: "But you never listen to what I say." She tilted her head back and closed her eyes, letting out a deep sigh. "You had it all with Wayne, and now look at this mess."

It was not uncommon for Mom to retreat to the past, and we would stay rooted there unless I could push us upward.

"I'm trying. I've made a few art contacts."

"What about a nursing job? A hospital would pay your health insurance. Aren't you worried about that?"

What I was worried about was failing in the arts. It meant so much to me to be trying. With the St. Alexius project, I started as a sapling. Then, for the past nine months, I was growing into a solid tree. At this moment I stood taller and stronger on my own, learning how to climb, successfully, too, not just by grabbing onto a branch with my hands, but also by pushing with my legs, using my entire body strength to thrust upward!

"Mom," I said, lifting her chin with my hand. Her eyes shifted to center on mine. "I want to have a life worth loving, deeply and passionately, and for me, it's not a nursing job."

She twisted her head out of my hold.

We fell into a silence.

The remainder of the visit focused on the boys, enjoying

their laughs and fun-loving shenanigans. As always, saying good-bye to the boys was the hardest hurdle. It actually helped that I held a prepaid, nonrefundable, plane ticket to Bismarck. The simple act of taking one step at a time became my destiny.

* * *

Twenty-four-pound Thanksgiving turkeys are huge, but that size was nothing compared to the first order I received from International, the company that sold to Pier One and Spiegel catalog. With one purchase order, I had 960 blessings for which to be thankful. That was how many petite art pieces they requested! However, that big contract came with an imposing deadline: thirty days! *How could I juggle it all by the end of November?*

I had been designing a kids' coloring book, too, for the Kirkwood Mall Medical Clinic, and taking more college classes toward a marketing degree. School was manageable, except for accounting. Debits and credits forced my artistically inclined brain to stay inside the lines. Ironically, it didn't take a balance sheet to add up to show I needed extra help to make the deadline.

After placing a *Help Wanted* newspaper ad, I found a couple of artsy gals, Beth and Bobby-Jean, to assist with crafting the collages. That was the easy part.

The hard part became deciding where we would work. Earlier, my apartment proved too small when I created 215 handmade holiday greeting cards for Mr. Carlsson in the bread-box-size kitchen. *Where would I put two additional people in addition to larger work tables?*

Although the apartment wasn't the most practical space in which to mass produce the mini-collages, it was the most economical. In order to make room, though, I had to pack up and move out of the way some of my belongings. Actually, lots of them.

I looked at my double bed. Memories haunted me ... almost overpowered me. *Don't let old thoughts be bigger than your common sense,* I instructed myself. *If you want to be able to move back to Michigan, scrimp and save wherever you can.* Suddenly, the apartment transformation became an effortless decision.

My teacher friend, Tina Weber, helped me out. We hauled the mattress, box spring, headboard and wicker furniture to her duplex.

Next, I contacted a local carpenter about building a pair of work tables. "It's mighty small in here." His broad arms stretched out side-to-side in the kitchen and living room, and they seemed to nearly touch both walls.

"We can butt one end of the table along this wall," I said, pointing to the area below the narrow basement window.

He measured and gave me a quote based on using unfinished 2-by-4 legs and Formica remnants for the top. Three days later the apartment was officially my art studio. The two hefty painting tables filled most of the kitchen and all of the living room. In the bedroom I wedged in a hide-a-bed couch and arranged a small coffee table in waiting-room style. For an office space I squeezed a folding table into a secluded corner. The room became an office by day and a bedroom by night. I was camping in my own domain, and the good news was I wouldn't get poison ivy there.

In the daylight hours, the studio flourished as Beth and

Bobby-Jean bustled about. We painted, crafted, packed, and shipped the first order with pride.

Several days later, the phone rang. "This is Ben in receiving at International Art," he grumbled. "I'm short seven landscapes."

How could he be short? We had dutifully counted thirty-two pieces into thirty piles. 32-30 had been our motto. I didn't question his count. Instead I asked, "Should we send the remainder?"

"Nah, I'll just deduct it from the invoice," he snapped and ended the call.

I melted into the folding desk chair. The lost revenue was disheartening. Nevertheless, I clung to the hope of receiving additional reorders. Then I could produce mini collages from anywhere I lived. No longer would most of my income be coming from the Bismarck community. That was the dream I had been nurturing for ten months.

When the payment arrived in the mail, it included a reorder! I flew to the phone and called Beth and Bobbie-Jean to ask them to increase their work hours, along with hiring two more gals.

The studio hummed as we adhered strip after strip of collaged papers. My workers were troopers, and their energy filled the once miserable daytime loneliness of the apartment. Quickly we became friends, and gladly I gave up the long hours behind my art desk on the college campus and began working on my assignments near the girls in the apartment. When they left at the end of the day, I headed off to attend my night class.

We shipped the next order in record time, and when the phone rang it was Ben, the International receiving specialist for our mini collages. "Your count was correct." Click.

The cottage industry not only hummed, it prospered.

A few weeks later, however, I would learn how volatile that industry could be.

The "girls" crafting mini-collages in the
basement apartment

Chapter 35
A Giant Step Backwards

The next day, sunshine seeped through the leafless elm trees, throwing black bars across me as I tossed a suitcase into the Chevette for a trip to Fargo.

I was on the verge of completing the community college classes at Bismarck State College. To complete my education I had to transfer to North Dakota State University in Fargo, the city due east, making it 196 miles closer to Michigan. I loved the idea of getting even a little bit closer to the boys.

Since Christmas and severe weather were approaching, I tossed in a winter survival kit of a coffee can crammed with a chunky candle, matches, flare, flashlight, and from a painting barter, a North Dakota specialty mini-pack of chocolate-covered chokecherry creams.

At the last minute Marge shuffled up and tapped on my car window. Her face peeked out from a fleece jacket. She tossed back the hood, and a mop of silver hair sprung about.

"I want you to have this thermal blanket for the trip. We could get snow any day. It's been unusually warm."

She waved the blanket at me, indicating for me to crank

down the window. "No, no." I didn't want to take her gear, even knowing she was right about the weather.

"Hogwash. You don't want me fretting when you're away." And with that, I gained an insulated wad for the trip.

The Chevette purred along on I-94 east toward Fargo. Mark the Mechanic had given me good advice. As long as I didn't jam-pack the compact with heavy art, the car hadn't overheated since the Big-One craft show. Faithfully I had been adding oil, quart after quart.

Two hundred miles later, I pulled into the North Dakota State University campus and parked in front of the Art Department, feeling confident. Proudly, I swung my portfolio out of the Chevette and marched into the building. I was ten minutes early for my appointment and eager to round out my knowledge in the visual arts. Letting the creative juices flow brought me a joyful energy.

"I have an appointment with Mr. Berg," I announced to a youthful blonde at the reception desk.

"There must be some mistake. Mr. Berg doesn't have any appointments today," she said.

"Could you check, again?" I asked. "I'm a transfer student from Bismarck, and the Admissions Department scheduled this appointment just before Christmas break. It's exactly one week from the day I called. We had even laughed about the coincidence." The situation was no longer funny, and my words came out in a rush.

"I don't need to check." She folded her arms across her chest. "Mr. Berg is never here on Tuesdays. In fact, he won't be back until final exams next week."

Hearing that, I felt hot, then, cold, then sick all over. I had just driven four hours.

"Is there anyone else who can review my art and give me acceptance?"

"Nope, only Mr. Berg."

I was at a dead end with this gal. I turned away dragging my art case with me. Once outside, something cold and wet touched my cheek. A snowflake. I trudged to the admissions building. As I waited to talk to someone, snow swirled past the window.

The admissions office apologized. The college had accepted my 4.0 GPA academic credits, but without Mr. Berg, I was at a standstill as an art major.

Shrugging into my winter jacket, I went out into the rotten weather. I was also in a rotten mood, but I had no jacket for that. Walking from the university building, the snow flurries had turned to sleet, shooting needle-like pricks at my face. By the time I reached the Chevette, my shoes were soaked and my nose ran. Shivering, I chipped a layer of ice off the car.

I had plans to meet my Bismarck college friend, Cindy Mueller, at her apartment for a quick lunch. In September she had transferred to Fargo. As I got halfway there, chunks of slush stuck to the wipers. Within minutes the sleet turned into a driving snow. I couldn't see more than a few feet in front of me. I inched my way into Cindy's parking lot.

"Cold?" Cindy asked, whipping open the door.

"Arctic is more like it."

"You'll never be able to drive home in this weather." Cindy knew I had a pile of work waiting for me in Bismarck. "You're going to have to spend the night."

My shoulders sagged as I realized I was snowbound in Fargo. I wondered how I'd make up for the lost time. The lost money ...

"We'll hang out. Watch a romance movie." She tried to make the best of the unexpected weather. "You don't have another choice. The Highway Department has already swung the gate," she said, referring to the no-nonsense North Dakota road safety rule.

For everyone's good, in white-out blizzard conditions, the highway patrol fanned out and locked down steel gates, closing off interstate on-ramps. With the flat terrain of the Midwest, nothing stops the howling winds of winter. It blows the snow with fury out of Canada and straight onto the American plains.

"You can leave first thing in the morning. But for now, let's have a glass of wine."

Despite Cindy's kind efforts, I felt like my heart had been stabbed with a corkscrew and twisted.

She noticed my sullen look. "Stop looking back. Remorse doesn't change anything; it only saps your energy and prevents you from moving forward."

I sipped the wine and let her wisdom and compassion comfort me.

The next morning a snowplow rumbled past Cindy's house. Bundling up against the elements, I ventured outside and fired up the Chevette. As I drove out of Fargo, the tires crunched on snow-covered roads. Although the sun peeked out and cheered things up a notch, nothing melted. The defroster struggled to keep up in the three-below-zero temperature. I hunched forward so I could see through the frosty windshield.

The surface of I-94 was packed, uneven ice, probably from the early sleet in the storm the day before. I could only putter along at thirty-five. At this rate it would take twice as long to get home, maybe eight hours.

At the crest of a slow incline, the Chevette spun sideways. In a panic, I sharply twisted the steering wheel, but the effort was useless. Head-on, I plunged into a drainage ditch, slamming into a mound of snow. The momentum jerked me forward, but I was unharmed. The engine coughed and died.

I turned the key, nothing. The motor was out cold. I sat paralyzed with the front end buried up to the windshield while the back wheels hung in the air. "Stay with your vehicle." Those were the safety words I remembered from Cindy's dad, Ed Mueller, Superintendent of North Dakota State Highway Patrol. "I don't trust that little compact," he had said earlier. "I'll have my crew keep an eye out for you." I knew help would arrive, but what an embarrassing moment. Anyone could slide off an icy highway, but I'd done it only five miles out of Fargo!

The interior temperature in the Chevette quickly turned arctic. I grabbed the winter survival can and pried off the lid. Marge's blanket caught my eye. Instantly I hoped this wad of fluff had some magical powers. But once unfolded, I discovered it barely covered my legs. Quickly, I spun my jacket backwards so I could breathe into the hood. Hot air blew back at me and I sucked in the warmth.

My mind began to wander and a shudder crept through me as the frigid air seeped into the car. *What was I doing stranded in a snow bank in North Dakota?*

As life blasted me with one disheartening challenge after another, I felt defeated. I wanted to pack it up and quit this "art foolishness," as some called it. I slunk low in my car seat as a bone-chilling doubt swirled around me. The uncertainty of the future loomed large. My elbow knocked the survival can and out rolled the pack of chokecherry crèmes. I snagged the frozen treat with my mitted hand and sunk a side molar into the chunk of rock-hard candy. A piece of chocolate coating cracked off and slowly melted in my mouth. I sucked on the sugar. It was a good thing the other supply of crèmes was miles away or I would have consumed those, too.

Surprisingly soon, a rap on the frosted window pulled me out of my misery. It was Mr. Mueller's road crew. They had the Chevette out of the snowdrift, the engine purring, and the car back on the road in less than an hour. I chugged into Bismarck well after dinnertime. In December the sun sets early in the Dakotas so darkness surrounded me as I dragged my gear into the apartment and flicked on a light. However, what I illuminated wasn't an apartment. It was an art studio.

Instantly, I could tell Beth and Bobbie-Jean, the crafty team, had hustled to get out the Pier One order for me. The girls had stacks of mini-collages ready for shipment to International.

This time the shiver up my spine wasn't from the cold or self-doubt. The studio reminded me that I was making progress in the art world. I felt my spirits rise. The drive to see if I could survive this "art foolishness" came back. Thank goodness I couldn't see the next roadblock waiting for me.

Chapter 36

Three Strikes You're Out

I could think of a hundred things I'd rather be doing on a frigid Christmas Eve than chasing after a wind-swept letter I had pulled from my mailbox and promptly dropped. Another gale was blowing, and the letter leaped over the fence into a neighbor's yard. I sprang into a jog and bounded for the gate out of our yard.

It normally took only moments to leave my back entrance, scoop letters out of the mailbox up front, and return. But I had been chasing this airborne letter for more than ten minutes. Thankfully it eventually blew flat against a wire fence. I hobbled across the crusty snow, snatched the letter, and headed back to the warmth in the apartment.

In all, I held three pieces of mail – and each held the promise of grand news!

Since moving to Bismarck almost a year ago, I'd been working at ways to generate income that would let me survive in the visual arts and finish my marketing education. I had conquered the small ways to pinch pennies, but any one of these letters could be the big break that I was counting on to make my efforts pay off. Which letter first?

- St. Alexius Medical Center
- International Art Concepts
- North Dakota State University

I picked the Med Center, fumbled with the envelope and ripped it open. *"... Sorry, we will not be implementing the Alex the Cat comic strip series ..."* In early 1990s, hospitals didn't run ads, or much in the way of marketing, so my thinking was ... what better way to promote St. Alexius than through humor in the Sunday funnies? Well, the joke was on me, I decided.

The second letter I opened was from International Art Concepts. I had submitted a new floral design to the company in a small "trial run for them to consider its merits." I hoped for a large reorder. I read: *"... Sorry, we are discontinuing your flower-branch motif ..."* The letter slipped from my grip and dropped to the floor. Working for the nationally distributed company was like riding a tsunami. Deadlines were fierce, often requiring me to suddenly increase staff and then, like this termination of a design, halt all production and layoff workers.

The letter from North Dakota State held devastating news ... *"Sorry, we will not be accepting your art major application at this time ..."*

I momentarily stood paralyzed, staring at the form letter with its chicken-scratched signature scrawled at the bottom by Clarence Berg, the department head of visual arts.

After the recent frostbitten trip to Fargo, including the snowbank mishap, I had followed up with a phone call to Professor Berg. He brusquely instructed me to "Submit slides of your artwork and I'll review them."

He clicked off the line before I could gather my thoughts and ask questions. Therefore, I submitted two dozen pristine slides of my work and a cover letter stating my interest to learn and grow under his leadership.

I shook the envelope. Empty, except for the rejection letter. He hadn't even returned my slides! I felt my spirits spiral downward and I crashed into the closest chair. All along I had been nervous about being able to earn a living as an artist, and I believed the answer to my success was to complete my education. But this letter changed everything!

The three rejection letters sat at my feet, which was where my heart had fallen. I had taken a risk leaving nursing and entering the world of creativity. It had been a risk of hope, one with the promise of something better. The journey hadn't been easy, but risk-taking rarely was easy. These letters certainly proved that.

Anger rose then, and I kicked the scattered letters. I caught sight of my calendar, the one with commitments ... and hopes. On the calendar were other risks I had planned to try, including airline tickets for New York City to exhibit at Art Expo in April.

As my focus returned to the present month, December, I realized next month would be the first anniversary of having my own business when I began drawing whimsical Alex for St. Alexius. Given that fifty percent of all small businesses fail within the first year, I was already beating the odds! I just had to keep going.

And I did. I circled the anniversary with a bright purple marker and then drew shiny gold stars all around it, letting the color bedazzle the calendar and my spirits. I had to focus if I wanted success at the upcoming Art Expo show. I wadded up the rejection letters, flung them in the trash and stomped the contents with my foot, burying those thoughts right along with the letters.

The December calendar showed another significant date for me: A long holiday break with my sons ... the best way to welcome in a New Year! The thought of my boys pushed me forward, until I thought of last year on Christmas Eve, cozy in Robert's Michigan condo with his promises and his gifts. *So much had changed!* Unavoidably, shots of despair and heartache penetrated my positivity.

Then I heard Marge's distinct rap on my kitchen door. "Are you coming upstairs? 'It's a Wonderful Life' is on TV in five minutes!"

"I'll be right there!" I called out. I didn't own a television, but it wasn't the TV that had me hiking up the stairs. It was Marge. She seemed to appear when I needed her most, just like the angel for Jimmy Stewart in the movie. I headed off to watch.

Chapter 37

St. Valentine's Weapon

Valentine's Day can be grand when your life is rosy, but it wasn't so peachy living alone and away from my sons. When I saw the return address on the envelope, I knew it wasn't from cupid. Letter writing was Wayne's preferred method to communicate with me regarding the boys.

As Valentine's night descended, an inky blackness lowered its way into the basement apartment, and I read the contents of the letter. Wayne wrote: "Dear Kathy, Brian is teary-eyed after your visits. Next time plan on taking the boys straight to school on Monday morning instead of dropping them off on Sunday at our house ..."

I collapsed into a chair, pulled out a journal, and wrote. It was more of a scribble as the pencil scratched at the paper. Self-doubt, remorse, it all came out as I scrawled for an hour as I tried to process this next challenge I faced as a long-distant single mom.

With the black of night deepening around me, I reflected on the path my name had taken. Mom always called me by my birth name, Kathleen. She thought the princess-like name was perfect for the child to whom she whispered stories of falling in love, marriage, and domestic bliss. Yet, in 1958, at the age of five, and starting kindergarten, Kathleen seemed too elegant for the tomboy whose doll buggy carried the neighbor's cat, while the forgotten Chatty Cathy doll graced the sidewalk, naked. The short and sassy ring to Kathy seemed to suit me better, and I insisted to my school friends that was my name.

As I headed into my teen years of chasing after boys, I lost that independent spirit without realizing it, but the name of Kathy stayed with me. Then, once in Bismarck, and determined to move beyond the symbolism that "Kathy" represented "bad mother" for me, I became Kate. The name was short and strong, and it gave me confidence daily.

I closed the cover – warped and wrinkled from other nights like tonight, when I wrote with a sweaty, shaky hand. This journal had been suggested by a psychologist from whom I bartered a painting in exchange for help with sorting through my feelings.

Months earlier, I was stunned hearing her first words to me: "Why did you wait so long to seek help?"

I was speechless. Since the first day that I found myself living alone eleven months ago, it seemed like I had been asking for help.

"Kate ... Kate." The counselor's voice snapped me out of my daze during my first session. "Let's move forward. Tell me a bit more about ..."

As she coached me, I found words and vented my insecurities.

"So you haven't left your sons; you simply have a different

schedule than most people," the counselor said. "Asking for help or admitting you're lost or overwhelmed doesn't mean you're weak. Opening up to someone is the ultimate act of courage and faith. It means you're strong enough to seek understanding. Resolution. I want you to keep a journal."

"Why?" I choked out the words, swallowing rapidly to press down the flood of emotion.

"It's very difficult for someone to see improvement on a daily basis," she offered. "But, later you'll be able to look back and see growth. It'll be reassuring."

For several months I had been scrawling in the journal. Surprisingly, I discovered she was right. I no longer picked it up nightly. Sometimes four days went by, even a week.

The braver I became in creating and marketing my art, the braver I became in depending on myself for personal power. I let myself get lost in learning and pushing forward.

Since those journaling days, I realized that facing regret and failure were huge obstacles to overcome.

* * *

It was a murky Monday morning in March the first time I dropped the boys off at school instead of at Wayne's house on Sunday night. I felt my chest tighten as I gathered the courage to grasp onto a shred of confidence that my presence was important to the boys, even though it was difficult each time for us to say our good-byes.

Before that visit to Michigan, I called Brian's fifth grade teacher to share that I would be dropping him off and saying good-bye. The teacher had been supportive.

I pulled the rental car up to the school. Kids frolicked,

enjoying ten minutes before the bell rang to start class. Adam bounced out of the car and chased after his friends.

Knowing Brian liked the details about things, at the beginning of our visit, he and I had talked about the change from Sunday night drop-off to saying goodbye at school on Monday. I made certain not to use "wiggle" words like *maybe, perhaps, probably* as the psychologist had coached me.

At the motel, I had already snatched my last hug. Brian didn't want us embracing in front of his friends at the school. With Adam off and running, Brian crawled out of the car with tears swimming in his eyes. He gave me a weak smile. The most I could expect.

He wandered away and stood alone with his back to the group. I saw his chest heave, and mine crushed right alongside although I was fifteen feet away.

Then near me I spotted Matt, a soccer teammate whose parents were divorced. Matt and his brother had been to the motel a few times after school to play Super Mario World with my sons. Brian was out of earshot, still turned away from the other kids.

"Hey, Matt." I called and he came toward me. "This is Brian's first time being dropped off at school after our visit. I know your Dad drops you off at home, but that must not feel any better," I said.

"No, it's not fun." He dropped his head.

"Maybe you could check on Brian in a little bit."

"Sure, no problem. I'll take care of it." With that, he jogged to the obstacle course.

I pulled the rental car around to a cluster of parked cars, hidden from the drop-off lane.

Sure enough, a few minutes later, Matt yelled, "Hey,

Brian! Get over here and see if you can beat my seven chin-ups!"

A challenge. It was perfect! Brian took the dare and hustled over. I counted eight pull-ups and saw the corner of a smile on my son's face. Even with that, my stomach felt like I had gone too many spins on a Tilt-A-Whirl. Tears streamed down my cheeks as I drove to the airport.

Later, as we had planned, I called his teacher. Brian had an uneventful day. That was the best I could do at the moment, but it made my goal to move closer to the boys all the more monumental.

Chapter 38
Unexpected Guest

The first Saturday night in March came upon me – the opening of my first solo art show at Elan Gallery. I was jittery from nerves, or was it just excitement? I wanted everything to go just right. For this event, Greta Johansson, executive director of Bismarck Art and Gallery Association kept her promise and executed a magnificent show for me. As the art glowed under the illuminating lights, the setting seemed worlds away from my cubbyhole apartment a few blocks away.

To illustrate my artistic growth, I had included a variety of media in the exhibit: watercolor, paper collage, oils; several larger than six feet. Their size made the room pulse with energy. My heart skipped as I gazed at my contemporary style that separated me from the majority of Midwest painters focused on realistic wildlife.

Less than halfway into the two-hour show, three red "Sold" dots already appeared on the price tags. I whirled around the room, glowing from the positive energy.

Among the crowd mingled a broad-girth man with more gray than brown in his hair. His back was toward me as he studied one of my oils. I saw his head tilt up, and then slowly drift down as he eyed the art. He moved on to the next painting and lingered again. Then he took a step to another piece.

In the hubbub of guests, I lost track of the gentleman until almost an hour later. By that time, he was at the last piece in his clockwise progression. My curiosity piqued. I approached him from behind and tapped his shoulder.

He turned around ... and I came nose to nose with Clarence Berg, head of the art department for North Dakota State in Fargo. I recognized him from his photo in the campus directory. His piercing, hawkish eyes penetrated mine.

"I'm quite taken with your work," he said. "I don't get to Bismarck often, but I'm delighted I was here to take in your exhibit. I'm impressed with your broken use of color."

I could only nod.

"I see from the artist bio that you're studying at Bismarck State. You should come to *my* school," he said, squaring his shoulders with pride and summarily extending a business card.

Clearly he didn't remember me, the slides of my art, or my application to *his* Department of Fine Arts.

I started to tell him the truth but reeled it back in. My application hadn't mattered to him. But it had mattered to me. I knew exactly how long it had been since I had scheduled that appointment, driven four hours, discovered Mr. Berg wasn't available, got stranded in a snowstorm, then mailed my whole application later ... only to be rejected by this man talking about "his" school. It had been three and a half months since his dismissal.

There was the whirring in my head from my blood pressure climbing. I knew keenly what it felt like to want something, to desire it. And it was not satisfied by Mr. Berg deeming me to be acceptable all these months later.

I thought how different my life would have been if he **had** accepted my credentials. I would have committed to living two more years in North Dakota. Instead, after living on my own for a year, I had a solo art show. Out of the corner of my eye, I saw another red dot tagged to a painting and felt an explosion of pride. Sold!

All at once, I realized I had moved on from the emotional need to use college as a form of validation. Yes, it had been a safe place to grow and learn, to be supported in trying something different. College classes ratified my decision to leave behind a stable job and paycheck for the exciting possibilities of a life in the arts.

At the exhibit that day, I was closer than ever to my goal of moving home. I still believed in learning and education, but if I went back to school in the future, it would be with Michigan residency.

Maybe a dose of truth-telling was in order after all. I looked Mr. Berg squarely in the eye. "I applied to your school," I said, locking my lips into a polite smile. "But I wasn't accepted."

He rubbed his hand over his chin. "Hmm."

I could tell he still didn't remember me, the slides of my art, or my application to *his* Department of Fine Art. I thanked him for the positive critique, told him I had other plans, and turned on my heels. Still with a smile, I let it all hang in the air and refused to let my mood sour.

At the end of the evening, I added up the sales. Enough for airline tickets to see my boys. And if I gave up new shoes, enough to gift them with two radio-controlled, turbo-charged race cars. Giving up the shoes was easy. My heart was in love with those crazy cars for the boys.

But when would I earn enough for a new car for me?

Chapter 39
Another Hurdle(s)

I wanted to join the ranks of successful artists Thomas Kincaid, Bev Doolittle, and P. Buckley Moss by getting into lithograph prints. It was a highly technical process of reproducing a painting by using a press that was capable of printing thousands of beautiful copies. It was a costly endeavor for my budget to hire an agent and an expert printer, but the end product would be a completely new income stream for me. With lithographs, the mainstream customer could afford a great likeness of the original at 75 percent less. The seller's excellent profit margin also made the product a perfect choice for an upcoming trade show. In April, I planned to attend New York City Art Expo, the wholesale show for gallery and frame shop owners.

Preparing for my big step into lithographs, I painted on the theme of one of my best selling images: robins on apple blossom branches. I did one large, focal-point piece and two smaller bird complements; they could be displayed as a matched set or they could stand alone.

As a next step I needed perfect photographs of the art so I made a second appointment at Larry Weller's studio in Bismarck.

"Welcome back," he sang out.

As in my earlier visit, I noticed Larry Weller's carefree smile – a pure, casual, beach-worthy welcome that reminded me of home in West Michigan and offered comfort.

Getting right into the shoot, he clipped up my art and clicked away with confidence and professionalism. It was hard not to like this man.

"Next, I'll have the photographs developed into transparencies and we'll proof them with Bill Serig at his advertising agency."

A name I recalled. Sixteen months ago, when I first arrived in Bismarck, that same Bill Serig glanced at my art portfolio and declared it was "too fine art" for his agency. So ... we would meet again.

This time, however, Bill took one look at the transparencies and said, "The art is mighty fine. Mighty fine, indeed."

Five days later I met Bill and Larry at Union Print Shop for the final step in the elaborate process of producing lithographs. Jim Bauer, the shop owner, nodded to me and then shook hands with Bill and Larry. Their grip was like arm wrestling. The three of them had a men's club going, and I was yet to know if they would initiate me into their group. I was here to evaluate the artist proofs, the first sheets off the press, but I was out of my league in this world of printmaking.

I wanted the lithographs to be perfect, but I knew it would take an effort for technology to produce a close replica.

Forty minutes later, we had tested five proofs and I had rejected them all.

"By now, we usually get this right," Jim, the shop owner, scuffed.

I felt the heat of the moment as this men's club turned into a pressure-cooker. I had scrounged every nickel to pay for this, so I certainly wanted the prints done right. Looking at the three men, I took a deep breath and stood my ground. "One more time," I said.

Jim didn't hesitate. He waved the technician to roll again. The prints came out star quality.

*Whispers in the Weeds, one of the two smaller
lithographs, edition of 650.*

I had been wrong before. In fact, if I was honest, I had been wrong a lot. But I had never been as wrong as when I pushed aside a certain little detail on my to-do list.

On big projects, I had always broken them into small, do-able tasks, taking one little step at a time. A brochure to promote the lithographs was the next small step, but it required additional money that I simply didn't have. When I budgeted for the printing, I had hoped some decent commission would come my way to pay for the brochures. I was wrong about getting a fresh commission. That had not happened.

Uncertainties surfaced. *Was my artistic talent a gift or a curse? If I could be content with nursing nine to five or, more likely, an awful night shift, I'd have a steady income.*

Then I discovered a local art festival sponsored by the Bismarck Presbyterian Church scheduled for late March. In a city without retail art galleries, festivals provided a chance to display art and possibly generate income so I entered the competition. With the success of my paper abstracts at the Elan Show, I would try that again. I started tearing papers for the project.

I focused on the décor color trends of the early 1990s – mauve and gray – matching a customer's exact shade of wall paint or fabric. Some art critics felt this was "going commercial" instead of painting art for art's sake, but my creative side enjoyed mixing paint in any color, for any purpose.

Opening night of the local event, I peeked around the portable wall units, and gasped so loudly, heads turned. A vivid blue ribbon dangled from one of my paintings! I'd won the first-place prize money! Better yet, I had sold all three pieces!

The next day I bounded to Serig advertising agency. For the promotional brochure we decided to use one of the textured papers I used in my new series of paper abstracts. The hand-stamped pattern made a perfect background against the crisp watercolor lithographs.

Implementing that concept meant another trip to Weller

Photography. Larry greeted me with his familiar, playful grin. For the third time, I'd watched in awe as he expertly captured my art under his powerful photo spotlights.

"These are interesting textures. Do you make this paper yourself? Does it take much time?"

The camera continued to click, along with a litany of other questions. I shrugged it off as idle chitchat. I didn't mind the distraction, as his lighthearted laugh made me join right in.

In the end, with Larry's photographs and Bill's design, I had a first-class brochure for my first wholesale art show in the Big Apple. I showed the promotional handout to Beth and Bobbie-Jean, my crafty team.

"Wow!" Beth ran her hand across the texture-like background that appeared 3-D from the depth. "It's dynamite!"

From her words, pride swooped in.

Then she said, "Did you get the phone message from New York? From event security?"

My confidence whooshed back out when I learned thirty-six hours before we were to catch the flight to NYC; event security informed me that the box of collapsible easels hadn't arrived. I had no time to replace the special-order easels, which needed two weeks to ship from the seller in Georgia. My art would be sitting on the floor! At the most important art show in the nation. With 25,000 attendees strolling by!

I needed to be noticed, but not like that!

Pam, my business-savvy friend, had offered to be my trade-show booth partner, and now her problem-solving skills were tested before we even stepped foot in the Big Apple. After calling many area companies that display at trade shows, Pam snagged several local easels for us to borrow.

Next we had to wrestle these longer-than-a-broomstick easels into a packing container. It took a lot of cardboard and glue gun creativity to create a secure box. Flexible air flight regulations of the era allowed us to check the cumbersome box as baggage. However, the long, narrow box didn't sail as smoothly through the cab ride in New York.

The driver swore in what I thought might be Arabic, but whatever the language, it needed no translation.

After all the challenges of getting to Art Expo, we finally arrived.

At the cold, hard shell of the Javits Convention Center, life buzzed with power tools as a small army of workers erected acres of elaborate displays. Many booths were a combination of three and four spaces. Highly-visibility corner booths had greater prestige and came with a premium price.

Pam and I hustled down the long aisle, finding our single, 4-by-10-foot booth wedged in the middle. We unpacked, assembled display bins, and set up the art. The paintings glowed under the rented lights. In less than sixteen hours I would be showing at Art Expo in New York! *What if I got signed as an artist by a poster publisher?* If that happened, thousands of my works would be printed and the royalties would roll in! Of course, the chance of establishing a relationship with a publisher was as likely as winning the lottery, one in millions, but I could dream.

The next morning in the dark shadows of dawn with the skyscrapers weighing down on us, I grew anxious. *Could I possibly sell any paintings among the hundreds of thousands of other art choices at the trade show?*

I shoved my nerves aside and settled into our meager booth as the show opened. We talked nonstop all day and into the night as a stream of convention-goers strolled by the booth. The strategy of printing the lithographs turned out well; we sold several sets. I had a spring in my step when we headed back to the hotel.

However, two long days later, at the end of the show, I had to admit that my publishing dream hadn't materialized.

"It's good business sense to appreciate any size victory," Pam consoled while shuffling through the stack of business cards we had gathered. "And I call this one a decent win."

We had made contact with interior designers and galleries across the country. The results of the show could dribble in for months, and the possibility of reorders held potential. I looked appreciatively at Pam and said, "I couldn't have done any of this without you. Thank you."

She waved me off. "You expect too much from yourself. Remember 'doing your best' is all you expect from your boys, so it's all you should expect from yourself." In the middle of the trade show aisle, Pam gave me a much-needed hug. Instantly I was reminded about Pam's most treasured attribute: her positive outlook on life. Surrounding myself around energetic Pam pushed me to believe in my own capabilities.

The thump of the clunky easel box falling nearby brought us back to the moment. "And as for this nightmare," Pam said, "let's ship it back with the containers. No more angry taxis!"

Chapter 40

Jitters

Although it was mid-April, I thought it was snowing. A second look told me the hundreds of fluffy white puffs floating in the air were the silky seeds of the cottonwood trees. I steered the tiny Chevette up the long drive of the North Dakota State Capitol, which towered 19 stories high – a skyscraper against the flat prairie. I followed a curvy side drive toward the Governor's residence to deliver a custom painting for the state's First Lady, Jane Sinner.

She had ordered the art for their personal space in the bedroom. The commissioned hollyhocks burst with soft pastel colors and fit with the traditional décor of the mansion.

As I uncovered and presented the art, the governor's wife gasped an appreciative, "Oh my!"

Hearing the thrill that radiated from those two words was the best response I could get. I felt lively and as light as the cottonwood puffs. Selling a framed, original work always helped my budget.

In a classic moment of bad timing, however, fewer than a dozen blocks from my apartment, scorched air shot from the dashboard of the Chevette and the engine poured out a dense cloud of smoke. Choking on the fumes of fried oil, I flew out of the car and stepped ten feet away to inhale a fresh breath.

From the side yard of a nearby home, a man rushed out dragging a garden hose. "That little compact is so hot it could catch fire." He blasted cold water at the car. The smoke turned to steam and the car hissed. Only minutes later, the kind stranger was towing me to get help. To Mark the Mechanic.

"Well, Kate." A somber expression crossed Mark's face. "I'm afraid that cold-water hose job cracked the engine block. The overheated engine was too hot for such a quick change of temperature. Sorry to say it, but you need a new car."

During the year-plus of living completely on my own in Bismarck, I'd come to know that anything could happen ... and that everything would. But that didn't mean I wasn't overwhelmed when it occurred.

It was a long walk home even though it was three short blocks.

In the corner of my "office," which became a bedroom at night when I unfolded the couch, I hunched over my card table "desk." *How could I generate the cash I needed for a new vehicle?*

Months earlier, I had filed an entry form for a very promising wholesale art event. It attracted galleries and framing shops looking to purchase artwork. The event was in the McCormick Convention Center near the Merchandise Mart in Chicago – America's third largest city, and 833 miles closer to Michigan. Chicago also had appeal for my career plan because delivering art from Michigan would be easy.

As I reviewed the application form, I saw an "escape clause," but not as in quitting. It was a possible way of getting the new vehicle I needed.

One of the professional development classes sponsored

by the Professional Picture Framers Association, the group hosting the event, was a five-panel open forum on "How to Write a Business Plan." They were seeking guests to fill the panel. And the position paid! All I had to do was speak in front a crowd of 500 plus picture framers on a topic I barely knew.

Over the past year, I'd learned that when nerves or fear hit, it was best to leap and keep learning. Since 18 percent of all Americans suffer from some form of fear or anxiety, I found comfort in being similar to nearly a fifth of the population.

I walked the six blocks to the library and stayed until closing to research business plans. Then I went back to my apartment and pecked out a detailed speech outline on the typewriter. In the early 1990s, Professional Picture Framers Association was the art education leader in the industry for galleries and custom frame shops, with 28,000 outlets nationally compared with 5,500 today.

In addition to income, getting a spot on the association panel would allow me to meet and greet some key players in the industry. Networking was a tool I needed to employ, according to my business plan research. After adding my credentials to the outline, I mailed the application letter.

Later that week fate arrived in my mailbox from an unexpected source. A national poster publishing company would be producing one of my floral watercolors in their next poster catalog! In the early 1990s this was considered hitting the big time in the world of art reproductions. *This could be more than buying-car-money. This could be my moving-money!*

Unbeknownst to me, the poster company had viewed my work at the New York Expo, and five weeks later, I had a contract in hand.

This was worthy of a big celebration!

Yet when I looked around the apartment ... emptiness greeted me. Beth and Bobbie-Jean had the day off, Marge wasn't home, and Pam and Tina were at work. *So who should I call?* I dialed my mother.

"Mom! Guess what!"

"Kathleen, is something wrong?" I caught her by surprise; I routinely telephoned only on Sunday mornings.

"No, no. Sorry, Mom. It's just good news. I received a publishing contract in the mail. A company is going to make posters of one of my paintings!" I didn't tell her I would be one small dot among thousands of images in the huge catalog.

"That's nice."

"It's great! This is my lucky break. I'll get royalties from every poster sold!"

"Is that like a paycheck?"

Mom didn't grasp the entrepreneur concept. My parents had experienced the Great Depression. Once Dad was out of high school, he enlisted in the Army during World War II. When he returned, like most men Dad worked for one company until retirement. My parents' beliefs were, if you had a job, you kept it. You got the dependable paycheck, paid vacations, and other benefits.

Mom's belief in working for a predictable paycheck escalated when I entered high school. She took a part-time job working mid-days in a local school cafeteria. She received a uniform allowance and contributions toward pension. She even received paid vacation for school holidays and summer breaks. I couldn't blame her for liking a steady job.

"Well, I'd better go," Mom said, keeping the conversation

short like she usually did. "You caught me peeling apples to make Dad a pie."

While baking made Mom happy, the poster contract made me frolic around the apartment for a week! Having inexpensive posters printed of my art was the perfect match in this golden art era of bargain metal framing.

However, the luster of the paint soon dried up with the publishing company. Ill-timed, the poster debuted at the tail end of the mauve décor trend and, with sluggish sales; the company never produced another image of mine.

Then a meeting with representatives of Duran Architects, Ron and Paul, gave me a lift. "Our goal is to secure one out of every five bids we submit."

One-out-of-five ... I was due for a win! I breezed out of Duran's office and found the victory in the mailbox. The Professional Picture Framers Association approved my application as an educator in Chicago. And there was a check!

I sped the seven blocks down to a car dealership as fast as my feet would hustle. Under my slacks, I let my knees knock in private as I hid my nerves. *This was a big purchase!* I chose a used minivan, negotiated a price, and took out a small loan. I kicked up my heels when they handed me my monthly payment book, proud to have gotten it all on my own! It was a Dodge Caravan, but to me ... a Cadillac.

In early May I hummed my way to Chicago in my shiny new-used van ready to speak at the early bird breakfast meeting of this two-day event. Upon entering the big conference room, I saw a rectangular table with a podium and microphone. I scanned the name cards. The four other panelists were men – a common statistic in this era of the early 1990s. Taking a second look at the cards, I noticed each person had

acronyms after their name, most commonly CPF, for Certi-
fied Picture Framer. Except mine. *Could I hold my own on
the panel?*

I was about to find out.

A stream of guests filled the round tables while the four
other speakers settled into their places. The first speaker hit
a few key points. When the next panelist spoke, his words
turned into a distant hum as tension curled in my gut. I
gazed at the door, wondering if I should make a quick getaway. *How fast could I pack up my booth and slither away
to North Dakota without anyone seeing me?* Before I could
decide, it was my turn to address the audience.

Standing at the podium, I saw a few heads that were
blinks away from dozing. I hadn't even begun my presentation! I cleared my throat and projected. The A-V tech flashed
my slides. Heads lifted. In a few short seconds all eyes were
on me. I had been the only one to bring visual aids. I rattled
off one quick personal story and summed up the core compo-
nents in fourteen minutes of the fifteen allowed.

It turned out public speaking was straightforward and
predictable – a vivid contrast to the rough and rocky road of
this artsy journey of mine that I'd been on since moving to
Bismarck almost a year and half ago.

After speaking, I was asked by the Professional Picture
Framers Association to prepare an outline to teach all-day
classes in San Francisco and again, in Chicago, at the next
trade shows. In addition to covering my entire transporta-
tion and lodging, the organization paid a speaking fee and
gave me an expense account!

Chapter 41
Getting Sidetracked

Back in Bismarck, the enemy found my weak spot and attacked. This time the weapons were charisma and a crisp business suit. I had my head down, working my once-a-month shift at the co-op gallery that had recently opened in Gateway Mall, when I raised my eyes to be greeted by a young man's easy smile. His thirtyish square jaw matched his squared shoulders that rested under his pin-striped suit.

He lingered among the paintings, yet his eyes followed me with a smile that was full of flirt. He sang smooth words about art in a bass note so low I felt it down to my toes. His flattery was heady and I liked the feeling. I wanted more. When our gazes finally connected, I found his deep and endless.

He responded to the moment of connectedness with a gentle tease in his voice. "My name's Rich Schmidt. I'm in town on business, but I hear Peacock Alley is a nice restaurant downtown. How about joining me for dinner?"

My breath caught somewhere down in my throat. I tried to focus on my job, but he scrambled my brain. Drawn in by his alluring gravelly voice, I agreed to dinner.

At closing time I locked up the gallery and drove over to meet him, feeling safe in the public space of Peacock Alley.

When I arrived at his table, he stood up and pulled out my chair. As he guided me into my seat, his hand touched my elbow and goose bumps popped on my arm. I felt alive. During an appetizer of the house specialty – cheese curds with bacon gravy – I ate up every compliment. Through the chicken gnocchi, I savored every kind word. While sipping brandied coffee, my voice had worn thin from talking, exchanging bits of my life for bits of his.

From across the table he reached over and, with one finger, caressed my chin. I slipped under his spell, loving every minute of his attentive ways. It had been a long time, indeed, since I'd felt this way.

I saw Rich every night of the three days he was in town. Thereafter he found ways to have additional sales calls in Bismarck. Before I knew it, he smooth-talked his way into making me believe he could run my small art company. Oblivious to temptation without realizing it, I was charmed into an old pattern of following someone else's commands to find my happiness.

After leaving his business position, he moved into my apartment. I loved the idea of someone with so much sales training taking over my strategies. I wanted to be successful in art, and I felt that Rich had all the right answers. After all, he had done sales in Jackson Hole, Wyoming and was familiar with Santa Fe, New Mexico, sophisticated cities with cultural and astute art galleries. In fact, right off, he got my paintings into the art mecca of Scottsdale, Arizona!

Feeling on top of the world, I bundled up seven original pieces! Shipping art with glass took a lot of padding, so the boxes were quite large.

Five days later I received a disturbing phone call from the

gallery owner. "I only wanted four paintings! I don't have storage for these boxes. I'm sending them *all* back, unopened!"

The setback was devastating. Worse, according to Rich, I misunderstood the directions and the incident was my fault. I didn't question my role and continued to cling to the idea that Rich held the solutions to my business success.

As time passed, Rich continued to find faults in my art and me. I took it as constructive criticism and tried to improve. In spite of my efforts, he continued to belittle my methods. Finally, when he scolded me for using a paper napkin to blow my nose instead of a Kleenex, I realized trying to "follow" his expectations was destroying what dignity I had left.

The word "follow" flashed in my brain. I had been down this road before, following first-love Donny to his college, then Wayne's engineering career to five states, then Robert to my current Bismarck home. I had chased after them thinking they had the key to my dreams. *How could I have fallen for this?* I felt foolish letting a man lure me into his way of thinking. My face burned from the embarrassment of falling yet again into an old habit. Somehow, I took that heat and turned it away from the shame I was feeling. I used it as power to ask Rich to leave.

It hurt, though, and for several weeks, I wallowed in guilt for making the same old mistakes. Then, one day, I realized I had done something I had not done in the past. I had said, "No!" I stood up for my self-worth and the belief that I was better than that. I had asked Rich to leave. Yes, it had been a setback, but in the end, I overcame a recurring weakness in my personality!

I barely had time to savor the moment, however. It was all about to evaporate with a single decision.

Chapter 42
Striking Gold ... or Blue

While May tulips bloomed, my curiosity blossomed when the phone rang and Larry Weller asked me to bring a handful of my textured papers to his studio. He had an idea. I had recently seen the photographer when he snapped pictures for my note card brochure – a failed marketing idea of mine where the only good thing that came from it was hearing Larry's rich, comforting, and contagious laugh. Wondering about his new idea, I toted a case of papers to his studio.

He flipped through the samples. "Is it difficult to teach someone how to create paper like this?"

"Not really. With a little practice it's pretty easy," I answered.

"How large a piece of paper can you paint?"

I shrugged, "How big do you need it?"

"140 inches wide."

Did I hear him correctly? "Almost twelve feet?"

"Actually 134 square feet. It'd be used as a photographic background to shoot portrait work. I think it would give senior pictures a fresh new look. More importantly, if we made a video on how to create paper backgrounds, we would have a winning product for do-it-yourself photographers. There's nothing available like this on the market!" he told me.

The early 1990s was a time before most how-to videos and a decade before DIY – the Do It Yourself TV network – debuted. It was twenty years before the internet beginnings of YouTube and Pinterest. At the time these painting techniques were still largely hidden nuggets of information.

If I was interested, Larry explained, the next step would be to meet two of his friends who'd help with the concept: a sound producer and a video editor.

"If we volunteered our time, we'd only have the expense of a small number of supplies, making investment costs minimal," Larry added.

It appeared there wasn't much to lose. On the other hand, if sales went national ... we had plenty to gain!

I discovered that there was a lot of depth to Larry Weller, and not because of his six-foot-three height. Starting in the middle of May, we began filming the how-to video. We were a team of four, yet the beginning was just Larry and me filming the various painting techniques. Video editing and voice-over would come later.

Before the first session, Larry phoned and shared the basic instructions. "We want this to look simple, so dress casually. And to emphasize how quick and easy the techniques are, don't plan on wardrobe changes. We'll film you in the same clothes each session so the edited tape will look like you're painting the same day."

No problem, I thought.

A few days later I met Larry at his studio and began unpacking and setting up my painting supplies. "Wait a minute, Kate!" Urgency rang in his voice.

I flinched.

"We need to film the very first step that a do-it-yourselfer should consider."

It was sound advice. These intricate steps were what the home viewer would appreciate. I screwed the lid back on the paint realizing this wouldn't be done in my dive-right-in approach.

"First we need to create a firm painting surface," Larry said. "I brought plywood sheets to lie down."

Following Larry's directions, I placed 4-by-8 plywood boards on the floor, aligned them side by side, and began duct taping the seams so the boards wouldn't shift. As I crawled on my hands and knees taping down the boards, I felt my knees sting, scraping across the ridged boards. He was right. This was a very "firm" painting surface. "Now, I brought trash bag liners to unroll along the perimeter of the boards to protect the carpet."

Ah ... another detail. However, I knew Larry's thorough plan would create a top-notch product so I was back on all fours, edging the plywood panels with the plastic liners.

Almost an hour later, I stepped over to my painting supplies and finally unscrewed a paint lid. I was ready for the fun part, dipping into wet paint.

"Hold up a minute. Before you start, walk me through what you're going to do first."

However, I hardly walked. Again I was down on my hands and knees. I pretended to pour paint and faked the sponge technique. My knees burned as I crawled across the twelve feet of paper doing a mock demonstration, but I kept a smile on my face.

Then I crawled again doing it "live" as he filmed. Inching

my way across, Larry had me occasionally pause so he could do close-up shots.

"One more time," he said over and over until every detail was captured.

Several hours later under the hot studio lights, I was ready to melt. My armpits were sweaty, my knees were numb, and I could feel my hair frizzing.

"Okay, we need a final shot of the completed project. Can you finish the entire sheet?"

That was 134 square feet! My body felt every 19,600 square inches of it!

I whimpered all the way home. One technique down. Five to go.

Chapter 43
The Bat Cave is Born

Although the calendar said it was the end of June, I was spring cleaning with a vengeance. Well, not just cleaning. I was trying to eek out floor space for my sons inside the small apartment. In three days they were arriving to spend their six-week summer vacation with me in Bismarck!

As I looked around the tiny space, I felt a sinking sensation in my stomach. *Where will the boys even sleep? How will this work?*

I opened the door that led to Marge's laundry room, which was just off the kitchen. I faced raw-wood stud walls, a cement floor, the hot water heater. Maybe I could convert it into a boys' "den." Still this would be so different from Michigan, where each had his own bedroom and a house full of amenities.

Wayne also provided a steady school-year schedule that never wavered from routine, whereas here the boys would experience my life as a self-employed artist. In preparation for these weeks together, I had scheduled all my business so I would be in town during the visit and arranged my work into half days so I'd have plenty of free time with them. Beth and Bobby-Jean would work in the mornings with me so we had the apartment to ourselves the rest of the time.

Somehow I shook off the fears and focused. Reality told me I had no choice but to attack this utility room.

I jogged up the side steps that led to Marge's kitchen and got her okay on my proposed renovations. In double-time, I began emptying, then cleaning, the utility room. Once I saw its bare bones, I realized that the room just might work. I borrowed a TV from Tina, hooked up the boys' video game console, filled the shelves with their favorite art supplies, rolled out a cushy rug, shoved in a borrowed futon from Pam, and pinned up a few sports posters. Outside of sharing the space with a washing machine, it was pretty nifty.

The next morning I was on a flight to Minneapolis. I had purposefully saved frequent flyer miles for this expensive fly-in, fly-out same-day trip. I wanted to meet my sons when their plane landed so they wouldn't have to switch flights with an airline escort. I was determined to make sure they knew every safety-travel tip and customer-service counter in that airport before they did this trip on their own for Christmas vacation.

As I waited in the Minneapolis airport, my stomach filled with turbulence watching their plane descend. The boys were seasoned flyers, traveling on jumbo jets to Florida for spring break each year with Wayne, but I stood on shaky legs until I had them wrapped in my arms.

Finally, I was able to yell, "Over here, over here!"

Instantly I saw the boys shrink a bit. At ten and eleven they were probably a bit embarrassed at my frantic arm waving as I jumped up and down. But I felt great! Whatever had been clenching inside my chest relaxed when I swept them up and savored the scent of root beer and salty peanuts – the snacks and drinks they had on the plane.

Shortly, we were boarding another plane to spend the summer discovering a new city, a new culture, a working mom, and "their room." I had my fingers crossed about the whole experience.

When I pulled the van into the apartment driveway, doubt made my throat tighten. The boys bailed out and Annie came at them full tilt, skidding to a stop. Instantly she gave a bark, eyes winking under her shaggy fringe.

"Hey, there!" Adam said, squatting down to pet the huggable mutt.

Annie affectionately slobbered him with kisses.

Then, from next door, Zach and Joey, two boys similar in age and sporting Minnesota Twins ball caps, strolled over. Before suitcases were even unloaded, the foursome were playing "Hot Box" – a backyard baseball game.

As for the laundry room, my doubts quickly vanished. "It's kind of mysterious ... like a Bat Cave!" they shouted. "What a great place away from grown-ups!" they sang out as they shut the door, chuckling about their privacy and firing up the Nintendo.

Exploring their postage-stamp of a backyard proved to be an adventure, too, spying on girls using my art face paint as camouflage. On ninety-degree days, it was off to the diving boards at the city pool or cooling off sliding in the muddy sandbars of the Missouri River.

Near the end of the visit, after a trip to the Badlands and some horseback riding, I had one more thing to show the boys: my video project in progress. Once inside Larry Weller's studio, the boys' eyes glued onto the enormous, 134-square-foot, seamless sheet of backdrop paper draped from floor to ceiling.

"Let's test out the background by taking your headshots," Larry suggested, camera poised to snap the boys' portraits.

Like typical kids, they moaned and groaned about smiling for the camera, but Larry clicked through their complaints. However, by Larry's fourth "just one more shot," the boys grew restless, reacting by placing finger horns behind their heads and smiles with their tongue touching their nose. Larry pranked them right back, giving them quarters for the pop machine that spit out mislabeled sodas. Through all that silliness, though, I ended up with some spectacular photos of my sons.

The way the boys blended into life in Bismarck that summer taught me a few things as well. The one I remember the most was a Babe Ruth poster they hung up in the Bat Cave: It's hard to beat a person who never gives up.

From the beginning I had been nervous about what the boys' experience in Bismarck would be like. Meeting the friends next door turned out to be better than I could have ever dreamed.

Ever since I made my decision, a year and a half ago, to fight for an art career and not face the shame of returning immediately to Michigan, I fretted about the whole situation. My moving-back-as-an-artist goal was growing closer. I hoped to reach it in six months, maybe fewer. Then I would return having accomplished what I wanted to show my sons this summer: That life was worth more than just living. It was worth loving passionately, even if it meant you had to break it down, pick it apart, and tackle it day by day.

Chapter 44

Looking for Every Dollar

Knowing I was just one big project away from my goal to move, I had to keep pushing. After my six-week visit with the boys, I was back on the video project at Larry's studio, smiling for the camera, grinning through the retakes, scooting on my hands and knees across the mammoth seamless paper, spreading paint, and following his every command.

Finally the six how-to techniques for the video were documented. Then he offered more. "Next, we'll film contrasting color samples."

I froze in place. I knew exactly what he was saying, but I couldn't get my mind to comprehend. Larry wanted additional samples in different color combinations. For example, if I painted the original technique in hues of blues, known as a monochromatic color scheme, he was requesting I make another sample using complementary colors – contrasting colors across from each other on the color wheel.

"And seamless paper comes in other colors!" He flashed his full-out smile as he pulled out rolls of paper in solid blue, green, black ... but I wasn't grinning.

Did this perfectionist want the six techniques painted on three additional colors? That was eighteen more samples, and if we did different color combinations, that meant thirty-six more pieces! I didn't think my knees would survive.

Then I glanced down at my turtleneck that I had worn each time to achieve "filming consistency" and realized it had been washed so many times it looked like the color of a dead fish, instead of the original pink salmon.

Trepidation set in, yet somewhere a ray of hope glowed inside me as I realized this could be my much-needed cash to get me home.

At the next session I don't know what made him do it, but Larry brought doughnuts. As I sunk my teeth into the massive quantities of sugar and shortening, I found myself jabbering about a business dilemma.

To reciprocate, I brought doughnuts to the next film session. I rattled off a chorus of "what to do, what to do?" as I voiced more business struggles mixed with my homesickness for the boys.

Larry nodded and listened. He oozed support, making me feel more comfortable than if I had bitten into the smooth custard filling of another Long John doughnut.

As the nights of filming progressed, I continued to talk about the pieces of my life. I shared my goal to move closer to the boys and fill my creative needs by starting a retail gallery and frame shop, like other successful owners I had met at the Professional Picture Framers Association.

Finally, after months of working together, all the samples and techniques were filmed. I thought I could sign off and say goodbye. Then I heard his chuckle, deep and throaty. "We need to film the introduction and the end with you talking live."

"Live?" I squeaked out. We had written a fifty-minute tutorial I would read from a sound booth and then Matt Hoey would edit.

"Yes, we'll create an office setting. You can sit at a desk with your framed art behind you," he said. "It'll give you and the film credibility. Wear something more business-like."

In comparison to the hundreds of feet of paper I had already painted, I was inches from crossing the finish line. Therefore, the next week I put on my business suit and an extra swipe of mascara to recite the few short lines of the opening and closing comments for the video.

That left fifty minutes of narration to master. Although it was early September and Tina had a new classroom of students, she made the time to coach me. Thankfully, her master's in speech communication had me "trilling" the dialogue. Days later, thanks to her persistence with my pronunciations, we wrapped up the script in one take.

Finally the video was out of my hands. At least until we had to sell the product.

A week later, at the video wrap-up party hosted by Matt, I sipped champagne.

"You seem a bit quiet," said Larry, who had strolled over to chat.

Instead of answering outright, I tipped the glass and took another swig, which was unlike me.

"Do you want to step away? Maybe go outside?" he asked.

I nodded and turned to the back door. My head was woozy from my three gulps.

In the small backyard of Matt's home, the western sun "back-lit" Larry's silhouette and circled him in "rim lighting." I had spent so many months around this photographer I had learned a bit of his terminology. I took a deep breath and for the first time enjoyed a moment of what had been an ugly day. But the calm didn't last long.

"You okay?" he asked.

"Yeah, I'm okay." But I knew I was a goner when my nose started to tingle, my throat started to swell, and my chin started to quiver.

"You sure?"

I shook my head and tried to blink the rising emotions away, but I made the mistake of looking up at Larry. His chocolate-colored eyes lingered and I melted.

"The Queen of Mean called me on the phone and swore at me today!" Tears flooded my face.

He didn't say a word. He simply eased himself onto the porch step and patted the spot next to him, indicating for me to sit down.

Larry had heard about my first icy meeting with The Queen. That was my title for Mrs. Duran, wife of the owner of the architectural firm where I freelanced. Since that initial St. Alexius presentation, my meetings were exclusively with Ron and Paul. She and I only nodded hello.

Until today. I dropped to the cement stoop. "She used every four-letter word I know." I felt my shoulders shake as I sniffled.

"But why was she so upset?"

His smooth voice wrapped around me. I wiped the tears with my shirtsleeve and took in a deep breath.

"She had a complaint from the Kirkwood Medical Clinic about my color selections. She said I ruined the entire project. Only she didn't use language you'd read in a Hallmark card."

Larry sat and listened just as he had done during the months we worked together, always asking about my day, my family. Rarely did he talk about himself. I blubbered through the floodgates. "She said it's an expensive mistake to fix and wanted to know who would pay for replacement materials! I've never heard someone so mad. This has never happened before."

"What did you do next?"

That was Larry, pushing me forward. He had done this before, like when I shared my homesickness for the boys, or when I struggled with an impossible art deadline. Larry always made me look ahead and focus on the next best thing.

"I told her I would call the clinic in the morning, make an appointment, and walk through the unit with them. When I think about it, I'm not sure what could be so grossly wrong. The color scheme is similar to the other units. The director was always pleased before."

His trick was working. The more I zeroed in on my relationship with the clinic and not on Mrs. Duran's reaction, the better I felt. The sobs had stopped and my breathing evened out.

"There must be a misunderstanding." Then he did it. He patted my knee.

I don't know if it was the touch, the champagne, or the emotional surge, but I blurted out, "I love you!"

We sat frozen when we both heard the words.

Then I wheezed, "No!" I floundered, quickly rising from the stoop, taking a step back. "I mean as a friend. You always listen. You always support me. You're so kind. You're my friend, right?" I was struggling for control.

Larry was married. Or he had been when Bob Serig intro-

228

duced us more than a year and a half ago. I felt flushed. Dazed. Confused.

Just then the back door swung open. "Hey," Matt said. "The casserole is ready. Come back inside and have some."

"Oh, I really can't," I said. "I need to get home. I've got a big meeting tomorrow." I darted away as fast as I could.

Chapter 45

To Worry or Not to Worry

"How are you?" That voice. There was no mistaking the deep mellow tone of Larry Weller through the phone line.

"I'm fine."

"You said you loved me."

I gulped. The gasp was so loud I knew he heard it.

Larry burst into a chuckle.

"You're funny," he said.

And just like that, all the potential horror of the three big words that I'd blurted out the day before melted away. It became clear to me Larry was my confidant, and he understood how I loved him as a dear friend. He was calling to check on me, knowing I had planned to have a serious meeting with the Kirkwood Clinic about my color scheme.

"It turns out Mrs. Duran was having a bad day," I said. "I met with the clinic director and walked the building project with her. The lighting isn't complete so the clinic is dark. The color selection will be fine when the project is finished."

"Great," he said. "So . . ." A long pause followed the word. There had never been an awkward moment between us.

Larry finally spoke, "Now that the video project is complete."

Another pause.

Larry cleared his throat. "And I know how you feel about me."

"Yeah, about yesterday ..." I said. "It was . . ." I groped for words.

Larry jumped in, "How about dinner?"

"Aren't you married?" I asked. I had made a mistake in my first marriage letting myself be swept away by Robert. Never again.

"Separated."

Oh.

"So . . ." he dragged the word out again.

The awkward silence was back.

"I'm moving to Michigan." The words came easily because I had been saying them for what felt like forever. And I meant them. Quickly my mind raced back to high school. I had followed my football hero, Donny, 620 miles to Michigan Tech University. I followed husband, Wayne, to Detroit, Duluth, Schenectady, Minneapolis, and then to Muskegon. I'd followed Robert to Bismarck. I finally learned I had been seeking my dreams in their dreams. I could not do that again.

My mind whirled. Larry was a commercial photographer, and all his income came from contacts right in Bismarck. His daughter was a senior in high school. He had history in this town. I could not, would not, let someone else have his way again. I was not backing down on my decision to move home.

"I know you're moving. And I wanted to talk to you about that."

I braced myself for the "It's all about my career" guy words.

Larry continued, "I've some thoughts about Michigan, too. Remember I told you I spent time in that state."

"I remember." *Where was this going?* This was not the normal business conversation we usually had. Nor was it a conversation about my troubles and me that had monopolized the hours of filming. Rarely did Larry talk about his life.

"I like Michigan."

"That's nice." I was getting more confused by the minute.

"I'm glad, because I've been thinking about moving there."

Had I heard him correctly? Yet, I knew I had. His serious tone meant business. I heard it in his voice. He was focused, determined. He had put himself out there. I couldn't believe it. This time it was about me.

"Can you come over?" I was too stunned to compose all the questions that raced in my head, so I just blurted out the invitation.

He laughed. That trademark chuckle. This time, as it resonated through the phone, it went straight to my heart and into my soul. I realized I did love this man. He was a loyal friend, and if fate had its way, maybe there could be more.

I brushed my teeth, extra-hard, swiped on some lip gloss and then jumped in and out of several sets of clothes. I paced three laps around the tiny apartment. Then another. Never before had I been nervous to meet Larry.

Then the rap at the door jolted me. Taking a deep breath, I tried to steady my heartbeat, but the rhythm wouldn't steady; it was as if it were trying to break out of my chest. I scurried to the door and tugged it open.

"Hey." He squeezed off a smile.

"Hi." I could only push out one word through my dry mouth and thick throat.

With his large hand he brushed back a whisk of his dark hair and cocked his head. Our eyes locked.

Somehow I found my manners, "Come in, come in," I stammered.

With his giant-sized stride he stepped into the apartment. "Do you want something to drink?"

On autopilot I turned and walked through the studio and into the cramped kitchen. Without thinking, I opened the refrigerator door. "You mentioned dinner. I could cook," I sounded too eager. It was as if I expected to find chilled white wine and the ingredients for homemade chicken cordon bleu waiting inside the refrigerator.

As the fridge door swung open, Larry barked out a huff of laughter. "You're going to cook dinner?" He stared into the refrigerator.

I followed his gaze. A lone orange, a quart of expired milk, a few lonely condiments.

"I'd rather talk ... because I love you, too," he said.

And just like that, it became clear to me that no matter how often I overlooked details, or got sidetracked or distracted, Larry had stood by me patiently during our months of filming. I realized he did love me. He loved me with the kind of love that included all my weaknesses and ambitions.

We stood in the toaster-size kitchen staring at each other, drinking each other in. The atmosphere changed between us; neither of us said anything. We just absorbed the emotion. He leaned in closer, and I got a whiff of the spiciness of a man after a hard day's work of hauling camera equipment.

He pulled me forward. I pressed into him as his eyelids closed and his lips dropped onto mine. All the strength was in that kiss. It burrowed into my core and I liked it there.

We pulled apart and that's when I heard it.

His laugh. Smooth and sweet like honey, coating me with comfort.

I brewed coffee. If I drank it, I don't remember. We chatted about his childhood in Iowa City, my youthful days in Detroit. We talked about his experience as an Air Force rescue medic in Vietnam and my days as a registered nurse. We shared sailing stories. He once had a boat in Iowa, while I had a day-sailor in Michigan.

Michigan. We discussed Holland, the city I had seriously considered for my new home. As we talked late into the night, I learned his parents were deceased, but he had a beloved aunt in Iowa along with five stepbrothers. His sister lived in California and his brother in England. North Dakota was home to his wife's family.

His wife's family. I could feel the words catch in my throat.

Larry sensed my unease. "We've been married twenty years, although she's more married to her family than me. Maybe that's why I've been attracted to you."

"Been?"

"I've had a pull for you since I first saw your photo on the cover of Fanfare." He was referring to the magazine that was tacked up in Greta Johansson's office at Elan Gallery.

"I never knew."

"I know. Anyway, Barbara and I should be signing papers any day. I want you to meet my daughter."

When he spoke the word daughter, I choked on my own thoughts. He patted my back with his broad hand, his touch gentle and kind. I stopped coughing.

"My daughter is easy to love." He approached the subject straight on.

I clung to my coffee cup and confronted him right back. "Are you sure you can say goodbye to her and move away?" I asked, feeling that familiar ugly knot in the pit of my stomach ... that awful ache in my heart from being squeezed in two. I knew what it was like to be without my sons. I wouldn't ask anyone to make that decision. This had to be Larry's choice.

"Allison is graduating and starting college in Grand Forks." In the same state but about 240 miles from Bismarck, Grand Forks is near the Canadian border. "Her life is all about her friends at this moment. I don't need to be near her to be close to her. Our relationship is strong. We'll never be far apart in our hearts."

His sincerity was so touching that I started tearing up and had to look away. I caught sight of my newest painting of a birch tree with its peeling layers of black and white bark. I had captured the texture of its craggy bark by incorporating rice paper into the surface of the picture.

Sitting in the kitchen with Larry, I felt like that tree. For more than a year, I had exposed the imperfections of my layers to him. He learned to love each of my flaws just as I had learned to accept them myself.

I don't think I ever finished that cup of coffee that day, but I closed a chapter on living alone. All we had left to do was figure out a way to sell our labor-of-love how-to video.

Chapter 46

Surprises in All Sizes

We were doomed – this group of four that had created the how-to video. As an artist, photographer, sound producer, and video editor, not one of us was the sales expert we needed to market the video.

Then, in September, my friend, Pam, decided to go back to college, leaving her full time job in business to become a graduate student. She offered to tackle the challenge on the side. "I think our best bet is to sell directly to paper manufacturers. If we can land them, we gain their wholesale customer base and even the retail end consumer."

That certainly lifted our spirits! The ripple effect of building a relationship with major distributors would be like snagging the entire sea of customers! Another benefit was that we could ship our videocassettes in quantities of 24, keeping labor down and revenues higher.

We gave Pam the nod to pursue Steller, the leader in the seamless paper industry. This family-run business since 1937 was interested! We negotiated a price, signed a contract, and fulfilled our first small order, which gave me a rush. This was my money from heaven! I rummaged through my closet, ready to start packing for home.

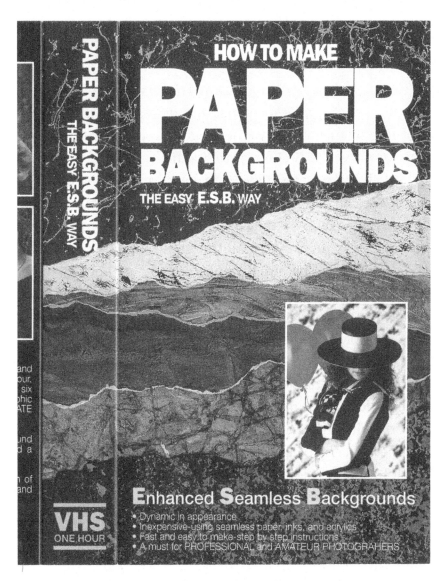

Front cover and spine of our how-to video

However, selling the video wasn't quite that easy.

* * *

The day was already too long, and it was only nine in the morning. It turned out we never got a reorder from Steller. Apparently we had set our price too high.

"Well, if we would have ..." I heard my own words ring in my ears and stopped myself. Would have – could have – should have excuses were never going to get me to Michigan.

Larry was drinking in all the knowledge he could hold about the art and picture framing industry, gathering knowledge from every trade magazine I had. His education from the top-rated Brooks Institute of Photography in Santa Barbara, California, gave him an eye for color and design. Seven years older than me, he was ready for a career change as he wanted to leave the physical demands of commercial photography, such as hauling equipment to each job site and perching on high platforms to get the right shot.

The concept of opening a retail space seemed to have merit for us, considering our shared interest in the arts. We also had a few statistics on our side: Nearly 70 percent of successful entrepreneurs had worked more than ten years as employees at other companies. Larry began his career in Iowa with the Des Moines Register, working a decade as a newspaper photographer, while I had my fourteen years as a registered nurse.

Thoughts of starting a business together brightened my mood. Once again Larry pushed me forward.

Unlike my previous relationships, I was entering this one after becoming self-reliant. It took me a lifetime to learn

I could count on myself 100 percent and follow my own dreams. There was nothing left to lose, and we had everything to gain moving forward in a healthy relationship.

I just had to find a different path than the how-to video for the funds to get closer to the boys.

The phone rang in early October.

"This is Dennis West, from US Healthcare." I didn't recognize the stern voice. "You gave me your card at the Bismarck Capitol Grounds Art Fair."

My mind raced to recall. That summer I had a booth in the syrupy humidity of the Minneapolis Uptown Art Fair and rushed to the rain-drenched Bismarck fair. I vaguely remembered a balding gentleman poking his head through a soaking-wet tent curtain and asking me for a business card. Could that sodden fellow be a VIP at one of the newest businesses in Bismarck? Nationally known, US Healthcare had recently built a large corporate office in the wide-open spaces on the edge of town. It employed more than 200 people.

"Can you come over in an hour?"

"Yes, I can." I felt overwhelmed, but changed into a business suit, fluffed my hair, grabbed a tape measure and leather-bond legal pad and drove north.

Exactly one hour later after the phone call, I walked into the reception area of US Healthcare. It overflowed with the contemporary furniture of Herman Miller, a leader in industrial design that had been founded in my home state of Michigan, making me instantly comfortable. I sunk into a stylish new Equa chair, the winner of the Design of the Decade award from *Time* magazine. It smelled like a new car, fresh and leathery.

Shortly, a receptionist escorted me to Mr. West's office.

Sure enough, there *was* the bald man from the art fair, but now he was dressed in a crisp suit and red power tie. After a few pleasantries, he gave me a tour of the new building to point out areas he felt were in need of art.

Back in his office he settled into his desk chair and motioned me to the chair across from him. He nonchalantly folded his hands on his desk and launched right into it: "In total, we need a quote for thirty-seven oversized pieces."

I clung to my chair to keep from flying to the ceiling. That would be a bid for about $25,000!

I was going home!

I had my work cut out for me, though. Dennis West said US Healthcare wanted wide wood frames that would match the modern Herman Miller furnishings. In a first for me, I needed to custom-make wood frames. I had been using pre-made aluminum frames I simply screwed together, using my one and only screwdriver from my bare-bones toolbox.

Thankfully, Larry had spent years with his hobby of building wood gliders. He owned vises, wood glue, sandpaper, and countless other gadgets to build the massive frames I needed. And build he did, meticulously gluing and assembling frames while I created massive collages for the new customer.

Our teamwork grew stronger as a haze floated in the air from his sanding and woodworking. We drifted through many conversations, marriage gliding in an out of the mix. There never was a formal proposal, just one night Larry asked, "When are we having the wedding?"

A smile curled across my face. "Can we wait to include the boys in Michigan? I want them there." I held my smile and waited.

He returned it with his deep rich laugh that always soothed my soul.

"That's fine by me. Just remember it's never too early for me to say 'I do.'" He scooped me in a big, reassuring embrace.

Then the phone rang once more. During my entire stay in Bismarck, I had steady work from St. Alexius and its satellite clinics but not once did I hear from their competitor, Med-Center One. Then I received a request to create ten pieces for MedCenter's reception-area remodel project. My work would be front and center in the second largest hospital in Bismarck. My money for the big move was growing!

I wondered, though, if my luck would hold when Larry met my mother.

Chapter 47
Meet the Parents

Maybe, just maybe, Larry's glowing smile could melt Mom.

In Bismarck, I had been struggling toward a career in the arts for almost two years, at that point, and was not about to declare defeat, but sometimes Mom could unravel me with one look. One word.

On the road to see my parents, I fiddled with the van radio as Larry and I approached Van Buren State Park. We were visiting with my recently retired mom and dad at their travel trailer. The Michigan campground where they were parked was about two hours out of Chicago, along Lake Michigan, and this was to be their final travel stop before heading to their new home in Florida.

The crackling static from our van radio's tinny speakers sounded like I felt on the inside: prickly and edgy about this whole meet-the-parents thing.

Larry and I had driven the thousand miles from the Dakotas for this meet-and-greet. Along the way we visited a half dozen galleries that carried my artwork. I had initially made contact with them at the New York and Chicago wholesale trade shows.

Over time, my relationship with them grew and they

invited us to visit and explore their operations. Each one had a frame shop and was run by married couples as we would be. Without hesitation, the galleries gave us great tips on store layout, inventory, and equipment. Their warm welcome boosted our confidence.

However, I wasn't as confident about the welcome Larry would get from my mother. I had already phoned her about Larry proposing, and becoming part of my moving plan.

On that scheduled morning the end of October, we rolled into my folks' campsite. Dad offered a cheerful, appropriate greeting while Mom stood in the camper doorway and nodded hello. We climbed out and Dad stepped up to shake Larry's large hand. As the men exchanged pleasantries, I slid up to Mom who was still standing by the camper. I heard bacon sizzling.

"Let's go inside and check what's on the stove." I stepped up to the door and steered her inside.

The bacon was officially shoe leather. I turned off the burner. "How about coffee together at the picnic table?" I suggested.

She nodded and gathered mugs out of the cupboard. I grabbed a tray to carry the coffee, and we took the mugs outside to a picnic table.

"Larry has been telling me what he's been learning about the picture framing business," Dad said as he and Larry gathered around.

Mom spoke for the first time. "I thought you were a photographer."

"We wanted to try something new," I offered.

Larry gave a full-fledged smile.

Mom pressed on, "At your age?"

"We're packing all my camera equipment," Larry said, giving his mustache a nervous tug. "But our real hope is not to have to use it, and we can sell it later."

"Can you feed four mouths being a picture framer?"

Larry rubbed his mustache again. If Mom kept firing the questions, Larry wouldn't have any facial hair left by lunchtime, even though I had shared with him that Mom didn't know much about small business.

"I've done some retail in a mall with photography. Owning a store can bring in decent money."

"And you plan to be a sales clerk?" She turned to me, eyes questioning.

"We have a business plan," I said.

"A business plan?" she repeated. "I've never heard of such a thing." She planted both hands on the table and pushed herself away. "I better go inside and check on the bacon."

A silence followed her as the three of us sat quietly.

"You know ... your mother has firm ideas about things." Dad got up from the table, too.

At first I thought he was going to follow Mom, but he wandered to his truck and fiddled with something in the back end. Thinking deeper about what he was doing, I realized that Dad was making a sound decision.

Time usually helped Mom process information. She had respect for hard work, so it wasn't the idea of us opening a store. Self-employment simply wasn't something Mom understood. I couldn't blame her. She believed in being loyal to your big employer for decades. It had worked for them. Dad's thirty years with Michigan Bell provided him with a bankable early retirement package at 55, a generous pension along with years of income from valuable stock. Mom also had a school annuity.

It would take time for Mom to understand my creative drive, and I was okay with that. I also realized it would take more than one visit for her to accept Larry; and that didn't faze me, either.

I savored the ease with which Larry had slipped into my life, and I knew someday he would soften Mom. My friendship with him was solid and our romance was flourishing. As my bond with him grew, I said goodbye to the years of loneliness and hello to the challenges of blending a family while starting a new business.

Chapter 48

Different Kind of Business Plan

It looked like a bowling alley ... this narrow, vacant retail space we were inspecting in the heart of downtown Holland. The West Michigan small town that, months earlier, had intrigued me as a great spot for opening a retail shop. The postcard-perfect little city sat seven miles inland from Lake Michigan's sandy beaches, blue skies, and soft sounds of the surf. It also had a core business district filling up with an interesting and dynamic mix of small shops and signature restaurants. My hope was to confirm the location with Larry because we were a couple and business partners.

Speaking as I stood in the empty space, I heard my voice echo off the high tin ceiling, "Well, the size of the space seems just about right for our business plan."

"Yep. We can build the portable wall right about here," Larry replied, tapping his shoe in the middle of the freshly renovated, 1,500-square-foot storefront with hardwood floors.

Laura, our real estate agent in tow, scratched her head. "What's a portable wall?"

Turning to Laura, I offered an explanation. "Our plan

246

is to have a back-up plan so we can adapt if our sales goals aren't met."

Then Larry added to my explanation. "We'd build a portable wall to separate the art gallery and picture framing business from my old profession as a commercial photographer."

"The wall would be built on wheels," I continued. "That way we can push it forward or back giving the most space to whichever business is flourishing."

Laura, probably mystified, politely nodded along. She didn't know us well enough to know whether we were serious and businesslike – or just plain crazy.

Larry and I exchanged broad grins. We took our business plan very seriously and put actual numbers to the details to ensure business success. Deep down I was delighted to have an alternate plan, no matter how off-the-wall the "portable wall" idea might sound. After all, the bottom line was this: Signing a five-year retail lease was a huge commitment, and not inexpensive.

"Besides the basement, there's one more level upstairs," Laura announced.

We trekked up the bare wood stairs. "This could be finished into an apartment!" I declared, wanting to skip through the bare-studs space, visualizing the potential for our new home.

"It'd be handy living above the shop." Larry threw me his signature smile.

"Where do we sign?" I asked, ready to seal the deal.

Laura riffled through a bundle of rental paper work she brought to the walk-through. After initialing twenty-odd pages of details, we placed our signatures on the final page. I wanted to loop my arm through Larry's and do a swing on the gleaming hardwood floor in celebration of launching step one of our new goals: featuring my art in our retail business!

Back in Bismarck, I cast my vote in the Bush verses Clinton 1992 election and returned home to a ringing phone at the apartment. It was Laura, back in Holland. "I just heard from Doug Earle, who owns the East Eighth Street storefront you want. Now he says he has a verbal lease agreement with someone else," Laura remarked.

My breath caught in my throat. All I could do was listen.

Laura went on: "I'm so disappointed for you, Kate. We signed all the right papers, but now he says he gave his word to someone else. How was I to know?"

The rest of the conversation was a haze, and I sunk to the floor, phone in hand. I don't remember how long I sat there.

Out of nowhere I heard a *bam, bam, bam* instead of a *knock – knock* on the back entrance door.

Then Larry flew into the apartment. "Your line has been busy for an hour! Are you okay?"

I looked down at the receiver in my hand. For the first time I heard the wail of the high-pitched dial tone blaring from the phone. Larry rushed over to me, placed the phone onto its cradle, and slid down on the floor next to me.

I somehow pulled myself together to relate the details of Laura's phone call.

True to his nature, Larry had me focus on the future. "So, this Mr. Earle is going to contact you directly?"

I nodded.

"Let's hear what he has to say before we close the door completely on that address," Larry said, threading his large fingers through mine.

After twenty months of living alone and making monumental decisions by myself, it was a relief to join hands.

Chapter 49

When Options Aren't an Option

It took three days, and a dozen Norwegian powdered-sugar rosettes, before the phone rang and Doug Earle introduced himself. It turned out he was part of the Prince Corporation family, who not only made noteworthy contributions to the Holland area, but also were also major downtown property owners.

"I'm afraid we're a handshake-kind-of-business," Doug relayed. "A verbal contract is as good as gold to us."

So just like that, Larry and I lost our twenty-page proposal Laura had compiled to rent the apartment/retail space combination.

Doug continued, "I'll have similar spaces available if you're willing to wait twelve months to arrive."

Reality slapped me in the face. A year! Our target date for the U-Haul was two months away. Larry had a buyer for his commercial photography business and had also turned down requests for future local jobs – ones that he couldn't regain after his refusal.

I was nearly finished with the US Healthcare project and

the last of my Bismarck commission work. On top of all that, Marge was seeking a new tenant. We couldn't wait a year to leave. To remain successful we had to meet our moving goal and start generating income as soon as we arrived in Holland.

"No, we need to arrive earlier," I said to Doug, staying firm.

"Well, we'll have a larger space that'll be ready in a couple months," Doug offered. "I can give it to you for the same rent. It has a basement, but it doesn't have an apartment above the store."

No apartment! I heard nothing except a loud whooshing in my ears. Somehow I managed to say, "I need to have my sons nearby."

"The college is directly behind downtown; there are a lot of apartments or houses to rent. I can give you first right of refusal when the next building with an apartment becomes available." His words were rushed. I think he sensed how tragic this news was for me.

"That means your five-year lease will just roll over to the next building," he went on. "I'd say we'd have a space within a year."

"Twelve months," I uttered. The words sounded like a prison sentence.

"If something comes up sooner, you'll be the first to know. In the meantime do you want the larger space for the same rent?"

For almost two years, I had worked to move closer to the boys, and I would wait no longer. Larry and I signed the lease on the larger retail space.

Still, sadness hung around my heart. I couldn't get the lost apartment out of my mind. It took all my energy to crawl onto my painting stool, and then I just stared into space with poor concentration.

The phone rang, waking me from my daze. I picked it up. "This is Valerie Haze."

Oh, yes. She was the local teacher who'd purchased my watercolors at the church art festival six months earlier.

"The circus is coming to town," she said. "They've asked the grade school kids to design a promotional poster. Our committee would be delighted to have you be the judge of the coloring contest. Please say you'll pick the winner."

Selfishly, I wanted to say no. I was content to withdraw and brood about the loss of my dream apartment. Then I felt a twinge of guilt. Valerie's loyalty to my art at that time had given me much-needed money. Without her, my getting to Holland may not have gotten this far.

"Sure," I replied, hiding my indifference. At the time I didn't realize how this experience would change my life.

The next day, while visiting Will-Moore Elementary School, I viewed hundreds of brightly drawn pictures of lions, tigers, and trapeze artists. I felt my spirits lift. My heart felt lighter as I studied the art and embraced the humor, sincerity, and honesty of the young creative souls. For the first time since losing the apartment deal, I realized I was focused on something/someone other than myself. It felt great!

For several days I had wallowed in self-pity and let it pull me down. Fortunately these kids let something deeper happen inside.

The schoolchildren's art added lightness to my spirit. It was the first inkling of hope, bringing possibilities and opportunities back to my mindset.

I happily went about the task of picking the winner, then

darted home and rang up Laura to mail us the Holland Sentinel Classified Ads. It was time to find an apartment and make this move happen.

Quickly my gaiety hit another stumbling block as Larry and I scanned the newspaper. We weren't just moving a thousand-plus miles; we were jumping up thousands in overhead expenses, too! Michigan cost of living was nearly twice that of North Dakota.

One apartment address, 11 West 21st Street, caught my eye. It was a two-bedroom upper flat of an older house, only twelve blocks from downtown. We could walk to work if we had to as we had budgeted for one car.

Laura sent us photographs in the mail. Larry hung over my shoulder as I thumbed through the pictures. "This must be the boys' bedroom. Val said it had avocado shag carpet." We stared at the wooly floor. Then I flipped to the next photo. "The kitchen is ... small." It was tinier than my current one-person basement kitchen!

"Yep. A broom closet, I'd call it." Larry snatched the photo from my hand and raised it closer to his face. "What's that yellow square stuck to the stove?" He pulled out his photography magnifier.

I bent my head alongside Larry's and we peered through the squatty lens. The note on the stove read: *Two settings – Hot and off.*

"I doubt we'll get home in time to fix dinner, anyway." Larry's laugh tumbled out. We both knew perfectly well it would be just the two of us to open and close the store, so we would be doing all the hours ourselves until we could afford to hire help. I stared at the photo. We were on a tight budget; there was no room to be frivolous.

"What's the next picture?" he asked.

I shuffled the stack. The bathroom photo showed a tub that sat on scuffed linoleum. No shower. The ceiling above the tub slanted at a severe angle; it looked as if you would have to hunch over like a football lineman in order to crawl into it.

"No problem," Larry said. "My motor home was smaller than that. Tell Laura we'll take it."

No wonder I loved this man.

Chapter 50

Passing Initiation

It all began, innocently enough, with a packet of Kool-Aid and a pitcher of water.

Brian and Adam had arrived to spend their three-week Christmas break with me in Bismarck. In the kitchen, Brian, now twelve, mixed up some Kool-Aid. Hovering nearby, Adam poked his nose into my fruit bowl and yanked out a banana with lots of black dots all over. Instead of peeling the over-ripe fruit to eat it, he twirled it in his hand like a six-shooter, and then I heard him snicker. "Let's make Larry a special 'welcome-to-the-family' drink and toss this banana into the Kool-Aid."

Working in the studio, I was within earshot of my sons' scheme. *Oh, my. This could be troublesome for Larry.* Then happiness rose up inside me when I thought of the recent cartoons I'd mailed to the boys before this visit. I sketched silly jokes about Larry and my growing relationship. Sunday phone calls with the kids confirmed their acceptance, laughing about the "big guy," as they'd come to call him.

My smile widened when I thought of the day before when Larry and I told the boys our plans to marry. The kids gave him Oreos filled with toothpaste. That had us rolling on the floor with laughter.

Seeing the boys' whip up their drink concoction in the kitchen, I realized pulling another prank on Larry was their way of bonding.

Shortly, Larry arrived at the apartment and chugged down his potion. Because he had caught a cold recently, it seems he couldn't taste a thing. The prank turned out to be on the boys!

After kitchen cleanup, Larry said, "Hey, there's a pesky fly in here. It must be a late hatcher." In one quick swoop he snatched the fly swatter off the hook from the laundry room, swished it through the air and smacked it on the kitchen table. "Got it!" With his other hand he pried back the tip of the swatter back. "Ah-ha. There you are, you bugger." He raised the swatter in the air to reveal a black dot. "Yum! This looks appetizing." He picked up the smashed bug and popped it in his mouth!

"Gross! You just ate a fly!" Brian said.

"Mom! You like *this* guy?" Adam asked. "He's crazy with a capitol K!"

Larry reached into his pocket and pulled out a handful of raisins. "It's hard to find a real-live fly in January."

"You faked us out!" Brian said and gave Larry a knuckle bump.

I couldn't wait until Larry and I moved to Holland. Yes, there would be challenges and surprises, but I wanted to tackle them all ... as a foursome together.

* * *

By February we neared the finish line.

We created and hung thirty-seven original pieces of art at

US Healthcare.

Ten original collages had been designed and delivered to MedCenter One.

Moving to Michigan was going to happen in 32 days. In one month I'd no longer be a thousand miles from Brian and Adam. I breezed into the Ground Round to sip a Long Island Tea with Tina.

After a few sips she leaned forward, got a serious look, and surprised me with an idea: "You should have a going-away art show."

I had never tried a stand-alone show before. When I moved soon, I would be leaving half a dozen paintings hanging for sale at the Fifth Street Gallery – the first gallery to open in Bismarck – but I had no idea if the shop would generate any income for me.

Tina pressed on. "It could be a final chance for the community to view a large collection of your work and possibly make a purchase. You could rent a hospitality room at the Best Western Hotel."

"Well, I do have the inventory, and I could certainly use the extra income," I said. "Do you think anyone would come?"

Tina choked on her tea. She gained her composure and said, "You have hundreds of customers, you know, in your Bismarck card catalog."

By card catalog, Tina was referring to my metal recipe boxes packed with index cards of customers' contact information. I had a box for every city where I'd shown in art fairs. The Bismarck box alone had more than 500 contact names.

This crazy idea just might work, I thought. Quickly, my mind was off on a tangent to Tina's suggestion: "I could design an invitation to the event, and Bobby-Jean and Beth could help me assemble them." I began sketching a heart theme on the napkin as Valentine's Day was ahead.

"There's one more idea that might help get customers to the show." A spark lit up in Tina's eyes. "Why don't you put Jack's and my name on the invitation, too?"

"That's brilliant!" Instantly I caught onto Tina's way of thinking. A host couple would add credibility, like a reference on a job. Tina and her husband knew hundreds of people in the community.

It turned out Tina's wisdom worked wonders. I had exceptional sales at the going-away show. It also gave me a chance to say goodbye to the many art lovers who had stood by me during my challenging days of growth in Bismarck. During the show, through the hotel conference room window, as I watched fluffy snowflakes fall, my thoughts drifted to how my sons had named such flurries "angel feathers." This time I knew the angels were the loyal folks of Bismarck who had watched over me while I was here. I couldn't have felt more blessed.

I could see my destination on the horizon. Then came a call from Doug Earle, my soon-to-be-landlord in Holland. "We're about a month behind on the renovations of your retail space. Can you delay your arrival?"

There was no way I could put off seeing my sons by a month. Not even a week. Not one day. Somehow I gathered my thoughts. In learning to improve my relationships skills, I realized I had to speak up and ask for help. A person could always tell me "no," but if I didn't ask, I certainly would never hear "yes" for an answer.

Caring for my sons had taught me a closely related lesson: *fake confidence to make confidence.* I told my future landlord the situation was time-sensitive. "We've given final notice to our landlords here in Bismarck. We can't put off the move. I produce wholesale collages and note cards. Is there a place we can work temporarily while we wait for the retail space to be ready?"

I got a yes!

He offered us a nearby empty warehouse to use.

However, it came with a trade-off. We'd have to move twice, actually three times if I counted the big move to Michigan. But who was counting? I was packing!

Chapter 51
Moving!

On the last morning in Bismarck, I awoke to a fresh blanket of snow. It felt like a fresh start – and it was! – as I drove the van behind Larry driving a 26-foot U-Haul truck with a 10-foot trailer attached, toting every possession we owned. The sun didn't peek out until eight hundred miles later, near Chicago. Then we had sapphire blue skies all the way to Holland.

The March sun warmed our car seats and our hearts. After months of saving and two years of jumping hurdles, I finally crossed the border into my home state. I held my head high. I had left behind my previous career and had successfully been living as a painter. I felt confident in my art talent and was ready to tackle the new challenges of being a gallery owner. Best of all, I'd be living only 16.6 miles from the boys ... not a thousand-plus!

We rumbled up to our temporary location on Sunday afternoon. Doug Earle, along with his accountant and four husky college guys, greeted us to help unload our U-Haul. Their hospitality made Holland feel like home.

Despite the endless work of settling in, we had to tackle sign permits, sales tax licenses, utility hook-ups, and more.

Yet I couldn't wait to walk down the aisle of our new gallery. Along with another aisle.

The wedding aisle.

It was important to me for the boys to be present at our wedding so Larry had agreed to wait, deciding to have the ceremony in Holland instead of Bismarck. It sounded easy enough until I learned we needed to be a member of a church, which involved an eight-week class. Presently sessions were concluding and the next classes wouldn't be until September, when school began.

Then things became more complicated. Muskegon County law prohibited minor children from staying overnight in the home of unmarried adults. All at once my unmarried status with Larry became an issue because when the boys would be coming every other weekend, Larry would have to stay in a hotel – an expense we hadn't counted on.

Since a church wedding couldn't happen until autumn, I called the Justice of the Peace. For a five-dollar fee, they'd be happy to marry us – but only at 11 a.m. on Mondays or Thursdays, which were school hours for the boys. I felt deflated.

Then I found an ad in a weekly newspaper: Are you planning a wedding on the beach or in a park? Rev. John Paul will perform your service at your location. Maybe John Paul could marry Larry and me at the gallery, I thought. The back courtyard was an explosion of rich spring greenery – the perfect place to say our vows!

It was the most encouraging phone call I made. Straight away John Paul focused on Brian and Adam. "Your sons are old enough to sign the marriage certificate and be witnesses. And during the ceremony I can include the exchange of keepsake gifts between the four of you."

His small gesture to include the boys in the ceremony made my heart feel lighter.

"May Sixteenth ... will that date work?"

My bubble burst a bit. That was my mother's birthday. She would not be at the wedding because they were not due back to Michigan until July for their annual summer camping visit from Florida. I couldn't think of a worse calendar coincidence.

The next morning I didn't know which phone call I dreaded more, arranging gallery trash recycling or calling Mom.

"Why can't you wait till summer to get married so your father and I can be there?" she asked.

I rattled off the custody laws.

Silence punched the air.

I broke the stillness that hung through the phone line, and said, "Since we're getting married on your birthday, we'll always think of you on our anniversary."

"Oh, Kathleen, you seem to make things so complicated." That was the Mom I had come to expect ... and loved.

Chapter 52

For Better or Worse

Ten ... nine ... eight ... The days before the largest tulip festival in America were slipping away, yet the to-do list to open the gallery seemed endless. Larry and I waded through a maze of boxes in our new retail space having moved from the temporary location over the previous weekend.

Six ... five ... four... the countdown to the festival continued. In the midst of this chaos, the front door swung open and a man about our age stepped into the jumbled mess. "Hey, there. I'm the guy next door, Jerry Ruisch. I own Classical Jazz." He surveyed the vast amount of work ahead of us. "So you guys are trying to open during Tulip Time?" He waved to the bustling Eighth Street scene behind him. All along the main downtown avenue, carnival concession vendors of kettle corn, elephant ears, and Dutch fat balls were setting up trailers, anticipating the crowds of people soon to be arriving.

"It's good money if you can open in time," Jerry told us.

We certainly could use the income. *But could we open in three days*? A sickening commotion started in my gut. *Slow breaths, Kate, slow breaths.* Somehow I managed to chat with Jerry for a while. Then the second he stepped out of the gallery, I called my friend Denise in Muskegon for help. She and her daughter arrived the next morning at seven. Working like an assembly line, one of us unpacked each item for sale, one hand-wrote price tags, and one tied them in place. They stayed until nine that night, leaving all our hard work sprawled out downstairs ready for display the next morning on Larry's newly varnished shelves in the galley.

By the time I shuffled off to the apartment that night, insecurity greeted me with a grind in my gut. *What had we gotten ourselves into?* Packing and moving home had been a goal for so long. I never stopped to ponder the monumental task of opening a new business. It had been six weeks since I had picked up a watercolor brush. I wondered if I had made the right decision.

Through a hazy sunrise at the gallery, I toted pottery over to Larry's new shelf unit. It didn't take long to realize I was in a fog when it came to effectively and esthetically merchandizing product ... another part of retail I knew nothing about!

It turned out I had nothing to worry about. The sparse inventory took up little room on the shelves.

Although we opened with as much product as we could afford, it took a lot of inventory to fill 1,500 square feet of retail. From the beginning Larry and I had a pay-as-you go philosophy. To avoid accumulating a huge debt, we decided not to pursue a bank loan. Just the thought of that 8.4% interest rate made me shake in my shoes.

We stayed another late night, and the next morning Larry flipped over the "open" sign. This was it! May 6, 1993, I had a thrill in my chest, but my stomach had nothing but nerves.

"Howdy! You-all got the Tulip Time poster?" A burly man entered and gave a quick scan of my landscape watercolors and contemporary paper collages.

"I'm sorry, sir, we don't. But I see a sign in the window at the shop across the street." I felt as out-of-place as this man decked out in his Texas belt buckle.

He tipped his hat and thanked me. All afternoon we had one inquiry after another from visitors seeking the poster. Each time I felt more and more out of place in this town we were trying to make our home. An art gallery should be selling tulip festival posters, but I had no idea how or where to even get them!

To help manage the flood of visitors/customers, Larry's Aunt Ruth arrived the next day from Iowa City, the town where she had lived for all of her eighty-three years. Because Ruth never had children of her own, her nephew was dear to her heart.

"Welcome, welcome!" Ruth greeted each guest – a handshake for the men or a gentle squeeze of a lady's arm. As she squinted at them through her square-lens eyeglasses, the top of her bouncy gray curls barely came up to their chins. She was that short. "Come meet the watercolorist ... and that's wheel-thrown pottery there, from North Dakota ... " Her voice ricocheted off the 13-foot tin ceilings, hardwood floors, and meager inventory.

Then in the middle of the second week, she rose on tiptoes and whispered in my ear, "Sweetie, since you're so busy ... I'll plan the refreshments for after the wedding."

The wedding!

It was five days away. We had the license. We had John Paul. We had new blue shirts for the boys. I even called Denise, who planned to attend with her husband, Roy. I thought I had covered the details, which I had. Yet, I never thought about a celebration for after the wedding on Sunday.

On that Friday I picked up the boys, just as on previous weekends, and headed straight to the gallery. On their other stays with us, they pitched in with endless store projects – a common practice in my small business. In Bismarck, throughout their vacations, they squeezed glue-guns to help make deadlines for mini-collages. During my school-time visits to Michigan, I often packed weaving projects and they helped me with those. Brian and Adam were a big part of my success in many ways.

However, on this notable visit to Holland, Ruth had other plans for the boys. When I tugged open the gallery door, Ruth bounded to greet us. "These must be your charming sons." She gave them each a playful punch on the arm. "You fellas know how to play Rummy?" Without waiting for an answer, she hooked an arm through each of their elbows and steered them to the basement. "I got us a table set up and thought we'd play a few rounds."

With that they were off, leaving me to greet and wait on customers. In between I hustled downstairs to check on the threesome. Each time, I found them bent over the makeshift cardboard-box break table, scooted up close to the card action as they squatted on lawn chairs. Impressed with Ruth's ability to engage the boys, I went back to work.

It wasn't until closing the shop on Saturday night I learned they were betting against who would inherit Ruth's 1978 Chevy Malibu!

On the day of the wedding, the boys slicked back their hair, slipped into their sharp blue shirts, and put on the khakis I had asked them to bring from home. They looked dapper. Then I glanced down and disappointment hit. Scuffed and worn athletic shoes poked out.

"Where are your church shoes?" I asked. I knew the boys attended church with Wayne and had assumed they owned dress-up shoes.

"You didn't say anything about shoes," Adam said.

I was angry with myself for missing another detail. I was mad at the boys because they should have known better. We had *talked* about the wedding for weeks! That's when I realized it. We had *talked* about how they *felt* about the wedding. "Tell me the inside story," I had coached them as I tapped where their heart was in their chest. This "tapping" tradition had been with my sons and me a long time. Suddenly, wearing frayed shoes to a wedding wasn't important. The fact that we were happy was important. All the tension I felt evaporated.

I swung an arm around them. "That's right; I didn't say anything about shoes." We headed off to the gallery to meet Larry and Ruth.

On arrival I caught sight of my soon-to-be-husband. His broad shoulders filled his ivory sport coat and made his almost black hair and mustache appear even more distinguished. He moseyed up to my side and whispered in my ear, "I do."

"It's too early to say that."

"Kate, it's never been too early for me." He gave the top of my head a quick peck and went off to greet the boys. My heart swelled, seeing the three of them together as Larry gave them some kind of secret guy handshake.

We gathered in the lush May courtyard behind the gallery and I took in the sweet aroma of pure spring: tulips and viburnum and love.

John Paul gave a nurturing message I felt had been written just for us.

When it came time to say our vows, a thought struck me. This time when I said, "I do," I wouldn't be following someone else's dreams. I knew in my heart that I could make it. I had the tenacity. I had the strength. I had my sons nearby and I had my art. And standing there, I counted my added blessing ... Larry.

We stood next to each other, side-by-side, as our thighs touched, forearms warm against each other and my shoulder pressed into his upper arm. He curled his large hand around mine, rubbed his thumb once across my knuckle and then cocooned my fingers into his palm. My skin, each individual cell, lit up with happiness.

After the sermon inside the gallery, I watched my sons scrawl their names as witnesses across the parchment certificate. Pride bubbled up and my eyes turned misty.

Then Ruth presented her refreshments – a bowl of mixed nuts. She gifted each of us with a paper cup and poured sparkling water. With a regal flair, she offered up a toast. This petite gal blessed us with not only her dignity but also her charm and wisdom. I couldn't have been happier clinking cups with my growing family ... headed for better or worse.

Our Wedding Day, May 16, 1993. Courtyard behind our first gallery. On left: Larry, Brian, 13. One right, Me, Adam 11 ... with "the shoes."

Chapter 53

Promises to Keep

I was living my dream – being closer to my sons. Although technically we weren't spending more time together, the more frequent visits ended with lightness when we said goodbye after our weekend. Then a different kind of tension developed.

Larry and I had our first argument. It could have been from working long hours, money only dribbling in, or the extra trip to Grand Haven for a forgotten band instrument. But it wasn't. Instead, Larry's tone rose when I wanted to take the boys for a trip to the video store.

"Will you cover the gallery for me?" I asked. The boys were restless after being inside due to an all-day rain, especially since there was no TV reception in the basement of the gallery.

"Kate!" he barked. "You took them *yesterday!*"

The harshness in his voice worked like a vise on my throat. Unable to respond, I turned away. Weeks earlier Larry and I had agreed to one trip a weekend for videos. I was breaking that promise. If I could have run away, I would have. Instead, I had to make a decision. I licked my dry lips and turned to the boys. "I'm sorry. I got sidetracked and made a mistake here. It's important to keep my word, which means no videos."

The boys shuffled away, both with lowered heads, and retreated to the basement.

The gallery remained empty of customers. In the quiet setting Larry's shoulders eased and his voice became mellow again. "I know that was difficult."

I put a finger to his lips and nodded. "You don't have to say anymore." As hard as it was to be firm with the boys, I had to admit my setback. Parenting would never be easy for me, yet in my heart I knew I had been wrong and needed to hold to the established rule.

"Look, it's quiet here," Larry said, waving an arm through the idle store space. "There's a pizza at the apartment we could bake. Why don't I take the boys there earlier than planned? A break from here would be good for us."

Watching the three of them leave felt right – including everything from before: the venting of angry words, the turning away and taking a moment, the apology and then this pizza compromise.

It turned out the days in Holland weren't easier than Bismarck, but they felt richer for my soul. It was a way of becoming closer to Larry, closer to the boys. I embraced these facts of real life with all of their pitfalls.

Then havoc swung a wider net. In addition to the boys' commitments of soccer, marching band, and other school programs, my sons requested adding an early morning paper route to our schedule. That meant we'd be hustling to make the thirty-five minute drive to Grand Haven at 5 a.m. in the darkness of winter with its slick icy roads.

I paced a loop in the tiny kitchen, muttering, "A paper

route would instill good work ethics in the boys ... it teaches kids the importance of dependability, punctuality and the handling of money."

With a gentle touch, Larry grasped my elbow, and said, "At first, when I had the photography business, I wanted all the fancy lights and camera equipment. There was always something newer, bigger and better that I was chasing. Then on location, I discovered there wasn't enough power to support such extravagance. I became comfortable with finding a balance. You'll find your balance."

I looked up into his brown eyes. They shined with support. Our relationship was so different from years ago when my poor communication skills plagued me and my confusion in the Colonial had overwhelmed me. Most regretfully, back then, the boys were innocent bystanders to my inability to understand and be a supportive mate.

It was a restlessness night of contemplating the pros and cons of a paper route. Numerous times, I would take a deep breath and try to center myself as the guilt of being a secondary parent edged its way into my heart, making me want to give the boys everything.

By morning, though, I told them that I couldn't take on one more responsibility and said no to the paper route.

Adam threw his arms in the air and yelled, "Hurray! I didn't want to get up that early anyhow."

"Yeah, it's fine with me, too," Brian said.

At first, anger wanted to surface in me because those rascals had put me through such agony. Then I realized with pride that I was becoming a more confident parent!

The next week, my life took a different twist. The incident happened when I needed someone to watch the gallery while

I was giving a lecture and Larry attended the Chicago picture frame trade show. The gallery had been open a couple of months, and the only person I could afford to work the gallery – meaning work for free – was Mom.

"Oh, Kathleen, that's not how I planned to spend my summer vacation in Michigan." The edge to her voice was crystal-clear when I called her in Florida.

One of our many times together. Summer 2013. Top Left: Mom, Dad, Me. Bottom left, Adam 12, Brian 13.

"It's only one day," I pushed.

All I heard was the eerie sound of nothing.

Finally, Mom said, "I'll talk to your dad."

My mouth slipped into a smile. This was Mom's way of telling me she supported me.

When the weekend arrived, I couldn't have loved her more; she ran the gallery side-by-side with the boys as they showed her the ropes of ringing a sale while we were out of town.

Chapter 54
Adapting

True to his word, fifteen months after arriving in Holland, Doug Earle offered us an apartment above a retail space a block east along Eighth Street. The Pooh's Corner bookstore was expanding to a larger space across the street. We happily made the move. Having the boys right above the gallery decreased my parental worries.

Then our kid-dilemmas had a different development.

Allison, Larry's daughter, had previously moved from Bismarck to attend Clarke College in Dubuque, Iowa. After a year of studies, she telephoned us.

"Dad, tuition and school expenses are more than I can manage." Larry tipped the receiver away from his ear, and I could make out the tremble in her voice. "I've tried every business and I can't find any part-time work. I don't know what to do."

Larry's eyes widened. We both knew Holland needed every worker it could find, as automotive and office-furniture plants had been booming with business. A surge of new restaurants and retail followed making us realize Allison could find work.

Knowing quite well what was on Larry's mind, I placed a

hand on his arm and gave it a squeeze as I nodded approval.

"Come live with us, Allison," Larry said after reading my thoughts correctly.

A move ensued, and she immediately found two part-time jobs that brought in enough money to cover her basic expenses. That left her college debt to face. Immediately I felt an ugly twist in my chest as a different kind of guilt pulsed through me. Larry had never hesitated to shoulder the added expenses the boys generated, even with the recent increase in my child support. But how could we afford to pay her loan?

We were several months away from our second anniversary of the store, and although sales were on the rise, most of the extra money went right back into the complex challenge of growing a retail business.

Adding still more to my uncertainties was this: How would Brian and Adam respond to our new family tenant? That night I couldn't sleep with my nerves too jangly and my brain too busy to rest. I lay in bed and listened to the nearby train whistles reverberate off the brick wall alongside our bedroom window until sleep finally came.

Waking with some resolve, I attacked our gallery budget. After juggling a few payments, relief flooded through me when I found a way to help pay off the debt.

As for the transition with the boys, it went as smoothly as watching them teach Allison how to downhill ski. They started on the bunny hill and it progressed from there. Soon enough, the boys began calling her their sister, and I was thrilled.

Also quite soon, daily life intruded, including her trail of dirty dishes.

"A-l-l-i-s-o-n!" I wanted to shout, but I had to bite my

tongue because the boys, at fourteen and fifteen, were good at leaving a bigger and uglier mess spattered inside the microwave.

Tensions certainly did rise, however. "A-d-a-m!" I shouted. "You slept through your dentist appointment."

In those not particularly touching moments, when I had to count to ten to regain my patience, I reminded myself that the normalcy of those moments was the win. I was grateful to be part of all three kids' lives.

However, I was not so sure they were grateful that I was part of theirs.

* * *

Frustration hit the kids hard. We were moving again.

"Business is flourishing!" Larry announced.

"We're expanding a half-block east to *double* the size of our retail space!" I explained to our trio.

I got narrowed eyes and grunts from my fifteen-and-six-teen-year-old sons.

Allison, although twenty-one, whined. "You haven't even been in Holland three years ... and this is your fourth move."

"We know, but My Taylor Shop is closing. It's the perfect opportunity," Larry said.

"It's perfect for *you*." The hushed remark was barely audible as it seeped from one of the kids' lips.

With the chaos of moving, we were having pizza for the third night in a row. That act was what finally made the trio break into smiles. It felt good to be laughing together again.

A few weeks later, unease lurked in my gut when I thought about the magnitude of juggling the demands of 3,300 square feet of retail. *Maybe the kids were right. Why had we moved?*

My mind raced back to Bismarck and my fear about earning a living in the arts. Larry and I had come so far, yet these escalated expenses had my nerves badly frayed.

From the beginning we worked as a team and split up tasks. That trick had made our business successful thus far. But we were growing beyond my safe space. Although I had learned plenty about retail/wholesale debits and credits, I knew next to nothing about sales projections. Passing the job off on Larry was no solution, either; he knew less about numbers than I did.

I heard the bell chime as a customer strolled in. I savored the distraction. When she made a purchase, I scratched numbers on our usual hand-written receipt pad, added up the sum and handed over her copy. Once the transaction ended and the customer had departed, Larry approached me.

"Kate, it's time to make the big switch to a computerized sales system. The software for our business even has mat board and frame inventory pre-installed. We simply input our gallery inventory and watch the magic as it generates information," he said, rocking back on his heels in pride over his research. "We can track our sales with accurate statistics and give up trying to guess about our way forward."

I was all ears. "I love the idea of learning an inventory management system," I said, recalling a new business method I had heard about called open-to-buy. "We can install the program to balance the buying of product with our cash flow." I wanted to tap dance with happiness, but then a new concern struck me and my feet stayed glued to the floor.

In 1996, computers were still prone to serious and recurring glitches. Already I struggled with our simple press-and-record answering machine. I could already picture our new computer freezing and the icy blue "screen of death" glaring at me. In the end, it turned out my teenage sons taught me which buttons to push in mid-glitch!

As we crossed over to our third anniversary with the store, Allison graduated from Grand Valley State University and began working with us full-time. I vibrated with excitement. Her ever-present smile brought brightness to each day of my life. Adding to my joy was the way she kept a youthful pulse on décor trends *and* a keen touch with our computers. Once again, I, this non-tech-savvy girl, divided and conquered our business tasks. With delight, I gave over to Allison our computerized inventory management system.

Chapter 55
Ups and Downs

I loved starting my day with the lure of creativity and uncertainty of what might happen next. Therefore, when the art business continued to be a spinning top, gaining momentum every year, it was thrilling, invigorating ... and a whole lot of work. The challenges notwithstanding, I savored every minute of it.

My typical day:

-Ringing sales

-Approving reorders

-Coaching team members

-Of course, swinging a paintbrush

Each one was a different way to express my creativity. Naturally, my favorite creative process continued to be the painting.

Often I used photographs for inspiration. It was rare that the completed artwork would resemble its model, as I got lost in my own direction for the artistic project. It was what I treasured most about letting creativity flow – the surprises.

Quickly my best-selling image became the birch tree. I couldn't think of a better image to represent me, because the tree was a pioneer. It was a highly adaptive species and able to sustain harsh conditions. It easily repopulated in clearings or damaged areas after a fire. It adjusted, rooted and then peeled its bark allowing itself to grow faster.

Like the birch, I peeled away layers to look inside myself, accept my weaknesses, and grow. Then I became strong enough to endure tough challenges as they arose. The next challenge, however, I never saw coming.

September 11, 2001. The terrorists attacks on America.

When the tragedy hit eight years after we opened the store, the gallery, the art industry, and the nation were all in for a bumpy ride. We all felt as if the world had shifted, and that purchasing new items, such as art and home décor, felt out of place in such a dark moment.

The Christmas holiday brought a bit more energy, yet not surprisingly, annual sales fell compared with our record high the year before.

In the midst of global chaos, however, the technological world continued to expand. The lithograph and poster worlds were changing by the minute. A highly technical, computerized printer replaced the traditional lithograph process that required printing hundreds of an edition. We purchased this "print-on-demand" giclee equipment and captured sales by reproducing a more economical yet highly accurate image of my paintings.

With the uncertainty of the economy, Larry and I felt a bit unsettled with our financial portfolio primarily tied up in the business and being renters for both our store and the apartment in which we lived.

Buying property seemed like a natural step.

In the springtime of 2002, we found a small house in Douglas, fifteen miles south of the gallery and three blocks from Lake Michigan. A tree-top room sat up on the second level, and I could see the tips of maples swishing across the window.

"That's where I want to be!" I said to Larry, feeling so blessed nine years later going from that tiny basement apartment in Bismarck to owning a home.

"Me, too, Kate," he said, ending with his hearty signature chuckle and sealing the deal for the two of us.

At our new home, the following August, with the air heavy from humidity and heat, I raced to beat the clock. Time was running out.

For more than two weeks, I had been painstakingly painting my entry for the 75th annual Tulip Time poster to come out in February 2004, six months down the road. In the summer heat, though, my deadline was only a week away. I was among five artists invited to submit works for consideration. I had lived in Holland for a decade and had never gotten this honor. The day the committee shared their interest in my artwork, I wanted to whoop out loud!

If chosen as an artist for this nationally prominent flower festival with its millions of tulips and thousands of tourists, I would go down in history along with the other renowned artists before me. I was determined to submit at least three grand watercolor choices. Yes, I had painted many tulips living in this city, but these new samples had to be my best work ever.

Tick, tick, tick.

The seconds racing by had me painting in our kitchen instead of the studio in the basement of the gallery. Wanting to work on the project all weekend, I had packed up a big load of supplies and brought them home. I dipped my paintbrush into the crystal-clear watercolor wash called Rose Madder. The tint was as soft as cotton candy, making it the perfect color for a tulip.

While I painted that weekend, Larry, newlywed Allison and her husband, John, splashed in the surf of nearby Lake Michigan. Even with the air conditioning humming, I could hear the roar of the frothy water from our home. Like the pounding swells, my head began to throb; I had been swinging a paintbrush since daybreak.

Just then the door flew open. Sand and sweat and the swish of sandals filled the kitchen.

"Can I see your masterpiece?" John asked.

"I don't have one ... yet."

John's jaw dropped. "What about these?" He pointed to the stack of seven or eight paintings in a heap on the kitchen table.

"For some reason," I explained, "I'm still struggling to get the best combination."

"Refuse to lose," John said in wholehearted support.

I had met John while Allison was attending Grand Valley State University. During the couple of years that I had known him, his coaching profession often inspired and refueled me. I dove back into painting with new inspiration.

By the deadline, I had three of what I felt were my best paintings ever to present to the Tulip Time poster committee. Then I had to wait for the verdict. During the day I paced my usual "worry walk." If I won the selection, an assortment of gift items would feature my medley of mixed-colored tulips, including signed and numbered limited editions, posters, notecards, magnets, mugs, T-shirts, and more.

Three days later the phone rang. They picked me! I had a

reason to celebrate! *Chocolate for everyone!* I scurried across the street, snatched the biggest bakery cake, and plunked it down in the gallery. Out came the party hats and festive napkins. Every customer savored a piece of cake, and I certainly savored the moment.

From my first days in Holland, the camaraderie from the people of this city had given me hope. This hope had its own life force of energy that had fueled me and made my dreams

HOLLAND, MICHIGAN   MAY 1-8, 2004

Tulip Time

75th Diamond Jubilee

My painting on the cover of Tulip Time brochure, 2004

come true. Being a Tulip Time artist made me feel grateful to be able to give something back to the community that supported me.

The next greatest honor came while I was telling my news to the boys. "You must be famous," Adam said.

"Actually, I'm just like you. I do my best, using the talent God gave me."

Soon, however, Adam's best stood to be tested.

Chapter 56
All in the Family

As our art business hurt from the ripple effect of 9/11, and a recession spread over Michigan, Adam experienced his own rough moment. In his late teens, he left Michigan State University and began working with a friend on home remodeling projects. Over the next two years, his focus stayed on construction. He also obtained his Realtor's license and even took the mortgage broker test. With the poor economy, though, he had a difficult path to follow in that field.

One icy January night I received a disturbing phone call. "Hey, Mom." He was calling from East Lansing. "I've been remodeling a big old house in Lansing on the bus route to Michigan State. Campus is just twenty-five minutes away, making it easy to rent to students. I have a chance to buy it, but I need you to co-sign."

He made it sound so simple. It wasn't.

"Adam, I know you're dependable, but the economy around us has been uncertain." I clutched the phone tighter as my hand grew slick with sweat, and then pressed on. "If you fall short on a payment, the bank can come after our house and business. It's too big a risk since I'm self-employed. I'm so sorry."

"But you've always helped me," he pleaded. "Like during my senior year of high school when I was struggling at Dad's. You let me come live with you."

My mind raced back to Adam's request, when he was seventeen. Although that conversation took place five years earlier, his words played like yesterday: "I feel trapped, overwhelmed. They don't get me." The memory haunted me because Adam's feelings back then were like the ones I had felt in the Colonial.

I talked to his high school teachers. After that, Larry and I agreed that it would be good for Adam to move in with us and finish high school.

"Mom? Mom, are you still there?" Adam's voice echoed through the phone line shaking me from my reverie.

"Yes. Just a second." I bit hard on my bottom lip trying to gather my thoughts. This request to co-sign on his mortgage had *Tonka* returning, pressing into my chest. *What have you learned Kate? How can you help your son?*

I had to practice tough love, which was still the hardest hurdle in dealing with my sons.

"Adam, you're a good kid, but it's too big of a risk. I can't sign. Is there another way I can help you?"

He hung up on me. Never had one of my kids hung up on me!

I began to question my decision. Was I giving him enough support? Adam was a risk taker. *Oh, my, this kid was so much like me! Was that a blessing or a curse?* At times like this, I didn't know. A shiver shot through me.

Adam was so unlike his older brother. Brian had held the same fast-food part-time job all through high school. Then, at Michigan Tech University, he became a civil engineer, and now was advancing nicely at his firm. He also had plans to marry his high school sweetheart, Lindsay Lawburg, that summer.

Yes, Brian's consistency was as natural to him as Adam's entrepreneurship was ingrained.

As my thoughts raced back to some of the art business struggles I had endured, I realized that Adam would bounce back just as I had over the years. From deep down he would latch onto another idea that would make him take a first step, which would lead him to a second step.

And he did. He found another way to buy the house, and soon we began talking again.

Bouncing back wasn't so easy for the gallery.

Michigan's sagging economy persisted and, in order to survive, we had to respond.

We tried expanding into a second retail space, but the new satellite location inside a furniture store never caught on. Despite our efforts, our art and framing sales continued to decline.

As I watched our portable art display walls be whisked away to make room for more shelving for smaller giftware items at smaller price points, a shot of anguish ricocheted inside me. I turned away, fighting to control my emotions. *Art is my passion. This can't be happening!*

The economic reality smacked me head-on as our open-to-buy inventory management system told us that in order to survive in this business we had to continue with smaller and lower priced products.

With merchandise arriving daily, displays constantly changed. Sometimes at three in the morning, I shouted, "Who's in charge here!? Me or the store?"

My echo was the only reply.

I admitted defeat to the retail space that was bigger than an outdoor tennis court. Yet as grueling as merchandising could be, I worked it like a jigsaw puzzle, making every piece fit.

Once finished, I stepped back and my chest expanded with pride. Small business was incredibly challenging, and it constantly filled my creative spirit.

Finding ways to diversify the gallery kept us on high alert. At a wholesale trade show, after walking mile after mile, Allison and I heard a gyrating hum. We edged our way through a gaggle of women.

"It's a customizing monogram machine," I said.

Allison twisted her tote bag to reveal the letter "A" centered on the front of her purse. "Personalization is the hottest trend!"

After researching, we plunged into the custom service. Sadly the added expense of a sewn monogram didn't excite our customers quite as much as it had Allison and me.

Next, we ventured into custom floral design. We blossomed with excitement about this new trend as Allison hustled off to a school in California. Although we had exquisite one-of-a kind arrangements, customers didn't flock to this strategy, either.

My spirits slipped a bit deeper during the wintry month of January. Annually we refreshed our thirteen-foot-tall walls by painting them in the latest trend colors. Sadly, our aesthetic efforts didn't seem to interest customers or spur sales.

Allison rallied and offered, "Let's try wallpaper! It's an up and coming trend."

Brian volunteered and straddled a ladder, hanging a vogue modern pattern. Almost immediately, the wallpaper company folded, ending our product availability and chance for profitability. Once again our efforts were for naught.

Pushing ahead yet once more, we hired a business consultant. At our first meeting at the store, he asked, "Where's Kate?"

"She's painting downstairs," Larry said.

"Well, bring her and her paints upstairs. Customers want to see the action!"

Larry beamed a smile of realization about the consultant's comment and wrapped me into a hug. "I love that idea!"

I caught Larry's eye and sprouted a smile of my own. For twelve years he supported any direction my creative spirit pointed. From his encouragement, an overflowing energy danced inside of me. I felt so blessed sharing this mutual support of each other.

After a decade in this location, we remodeled the store, most significantly adding a painting studio for me right in the front window! I never minded working in the lower level, but by leaving the small and closed off space, for the first time in a long time I let my oil paints fly! How delightful to dust off my palette knife, mix my lush oil pigments, and let the tartness of turpentine hover in the air.

Painting upstairs, in full public view, reminded me that change could be a good thing. Sometimes.

* * *

My feelings changed when I heard his cry. Up until that very moment, I felt too young to be a grandmother. I'd only been a shopkeeper for thirteen years, and I felt there was still so much to learn about that. However, in 2006, when Allison and John had a baby boy, Jackson, and I snuggled him, any uncertainties about being Grandma melted away.

The next year Jackson got a sister, Lilly. While I was immersed in the frantic pace of these toddlers, bouncing from playing dress-up to stringing Cheerios, John, the teacher/coach, threw us a curve ball.

Restless to explore, John announced he had been offered his "dream" job in Austin, Texas. Six states away and too many miles to count!

Their house sold in one day, and they packed a U-Haul before I could blink. In what seemed like overnight, John rumbled out of town with all their belongings while Allison wrapped up her work commitments at the gallery.

I lost all focus as sadness melted my heart. There was no underestimating the inspiration Allison brought into my life, after fifteen years of her inspired assistance. She encouraged me in art, made joint buying decisions for gallery goods, and added immeasurably to all our family gatherings. Through tears, I managed to stuff car games and surprises into a variety of travel-treat bags for my grand-toddlers to open during their long drive.

The next day I picked up the ringing gallery phone.

"Kate, it's John." His voice sounded strained and raw.

I sunk into a chair. He never called me. Through the phone line I heard him take in a deep and clearly emotion-laden breath. "What's wrong?" I asked.

"I'm in Texas. The job isn't at all what they promised. I don't know what to do." Then, between choking sounds, he broke into a distraught soul-baring: "I've made such a mess of things. Allison is only a couple days behind me in driving out here, but there won't be the money I had planned. I'm so ashamed. I jumped too fast and made a foolish mistake ..."

Although it had been years, instantly *Tonka* was back crushing my chest as my mind raced back in time. Those were the same words I had uttered when I was left suddenly alone in Bismarck: *shame, mistake, foolish.* The fear from them all rushed back.

"What should I do, Kate? It's so embarrassing," John continued. "I don't know if I can face my old friends. I think something like this happened to you once, didn't it?"

My old regret from Bismarck rose up. Many times over the years, when I looked back on that time, I wished that I had swallowed my pride, tucked away my ego, and returned to Michigan sooner. Misgivings plagued me for being so weak that I couldn't face my disgrace.

But the truth was this: I felt I had no one to turn to, and I allowed my scandal to influence my decision. Somehow I had to take that experience and help John on the spot.

From deep inside I pulled up as much courage as I could gather. "Are you certain the job is wrong for you?"

"It is," his voice croaked.

"Then that is where you have to start. Do you like Michigan enough to come back?"

"I do, but I'm just so humiliated."

"John, your old friends will forget, especially since this decision brings them no personal hardship. Remember Larry and I love you no matter what you decide. Talk to Allison. Somehow things will work out."

John clicked off.

They moved back to Michigan, John returned to college for his master's degree, Allison rejoined the team, and I snatched all four of them into the biggest hug I could give them.

Reuniting with family wasn't my only blessing.

Chapter 57

Never Ending Changes

Times got tougher as the Michigan economy continued to struggle so I was thrilled when an online, print-on-demand company requested samples of my paintings. Before submitting the images, I repainted each piece several times to assure I submitted the best work I was capable of producing.

Later, Larry actually giggled when I danced a jig as I told him, "They published eighteen of my pieces! I feel so honored to be one of the artists on their web site!"

It didn't faze me that his chuckle, usually a bit gritty, turned into a tee-hee-hee, girl-like twitter as he watched my feet do a silly shuffle to music I heard only in my head. My art was on-line!

Sadly, our production costs in the venture escalated, and it made better business sense to part ways with the company.

I wasn't the only one having a setback.

When the subprime mortgage crisis hit in 2007, Adam was scraping to barely make his house payments. Luckily, the next year he found an investor to purchase the home. With his newfound freedom, he called once more.

"Mom, I'm buying a one-way ticket to California!"

Although my chest ached, I knew I had to let him go. Michigan's deeply troubled job market only held uncertainty for Adam. He left, giving his handyman tools to his brother and donating his computer. With a single backpack slung over a shoulder, he left with a smile as wide as the Pacific Ocean.

The changes kept coming.

Facebook, Instagram, Twitter, Pinterest. They were all buzzwords of business changing my traditional newspaper and snail-mail advertising strategies of the past twenty years. By 2012, online shopping was predicted to make up one-third of all retail consumption.

The sales of my art stayed strong as customers requested unframed oil on canvas instead of my beloved watercolors that required the added cost of a picture frame. The canvas sales kept me painting, and at the end of the day, when I spread my fingers wide, I took notice. If I saw paint wedged under my fingernails ... that made it the best day ever!

Even though I loved the texture of using a palette knife with oils, the technique became repetitive. I began to crave other inspiration.

Restless, I pursued an interest I had percolating for a long time – to become an author.

Nestled among old photo albums were copies of the one-page short stories and cartoons I had written to my sons about their youthful adventures. I had dreamed of one day turning them into a book to share with my grandchildren. Then in 2010, when Brian and Lindsay were expecting their first child, I decided it was time!

As I sorted the stories, yellowed after seventeen years, my

mind raced back to so many years earlier when I'd left nursing to wield a paintbrush. Like then, I didn't want to regret not trying.

For encouragement, I went in search of Larry. "I'm starting a new hobby," I said.

He cocked his head with a quizzical look.

Over the years he never knew in what direction I might go so I shared a bit more: "I'm going to write that book about the boys that I've always talked about, focusing on the times we went summer camping. The kids were younger and did silly things like getting me to eat their burnt campfire marshmallows. Can you believe they tricked me into believing they were full of vitamins?"

A smile spread across his face and he said, "I like it. Get started."

Truthfully, it was the answer I expected. My husband always supported my ambitions. It didn't matter if I failed or succeeded, he encouraged me to explore. Once more, he reminded me of how lucky I was to be in a healthy relationship where we supported one another.

While I drew up an outline, a thrill quickened my heart yet my head told me I had a lot to learn. Rules of grammar were foggy. Even worse, I had gotten a "C" in high school English, never quite understanding plot, theme, or symbolism along with other elements of an author's craft.

I trotted off to the library for some how-to help on writing children's fiction. I studied and hit the laptop keys for months. I yearned to make my sons smile at my musings. I wanted to take our happy times as family and pass them on in written pages for my grandchildren, but I was pointed 360 degrees out of my comfort zone!

Tackling this first draft alone would constitute a small victory. Next I had to rally the courage to have my writing critiqued. As I chattered on the inside, I asked an editor friend from The Grand Rapids Press to look over my work. Sure enough, not one page came back without a red mark!

The constructive criticism gave me momentum and I pressed on. After each edit, from one professional after another, the writing improved. What a thrill for me!

While I plugged away at learning point-of-view and the three-dimensional aspects of character development, my mom and dad tackled a different challenge.

* * *

The plane landed, but there was no one there to greet us in Florida.

"That's odd," I said to Larry. "Mom said she and Dad would be here." Perspiration sprouted on my forehead, not only from the instant humid haze of the eighty-degree temperature, but from the unease brewing in my gut about my parents' tardiness.

"Your dad is never late," Larry said, not realizing this didn't help my trepidations.

"Hello, there!"

I turned my head toward the greeting. One of my parents' neighbors, Brenda Secor, waved an arm high in the air.

"Your dad has taken a fall, but he's resting easy. I came instead to pick you up." I felt fortunate my parents had supportive neighbors at the retirement community where they lived.

We hitched a ride with Brenda and soon found my dad

propped up in his recliner, with Mom doting on his every need. Dad was eighty-seven, and his health had started to decline. He walked with a cane, and his beloved crossword puzzle now sat idle on the end table, yet we still had a loving visit.

Once home, and back to business, I continued my writing whenever I could spare a chunk of time. It took more than three years of learning before my first manuscript was ready for publication.

As in the painting and art business, technology had changed the publishing industry, too. My writing coaches seemed to agree on two choices: to seek a book agent or to self-publish. The latter appealed to my impulsive nature, and I liked the idea of having a new product to feature in the gallery. Newness always brought energy to the store so I chose the quicker self-publishing route.

As with most projects, the learning curve of self-publishing hit a few snags. Even as I approached my sixtieth birthday, which sounded so much older than fifty-something, I was mesmerized by the excitement of trying something new. *Beached in a Camper* launched in June 2013.

Brian's copy sits neatly on their family bookshelf. Adam's response to the gift book was ... all Adam: "I'm so proud that it's a book about me that I gave it to my girlfriend." *Why wasn't I surprised Adam didn't hang onto his?*

Mom proudly read her book, but sadly Dad had passed away.

After his death, Mom stayed independent in Florida until she lost her driver's license. Feeling isolated, she telephoned.

"I'm going to live in a senior center about forty minutes from Gregg." She referred to my older, retired bachelor brother who lived four hours away from me in rural northern Michigan. "He has time for me. You're too busy, Kathleen."

Long ago, I learned Mom's intentions were to protect me. Besides, working full time at the gallery did keep me busy. However, in the end, Greg and I decided it best for her to live closer to me. We got her settled at The Warm Friend Independent Living Center, right across from the gallery in downtown Holland.

Soon after, at eighty-seven using her walker, she strolled into the gallery and said, "Oh, Kathleen. I met another friend. I told her you're my daughter and, like everyone else, she knew all about Moynihan Gallery!"

Mom spun around on her walker and rolled out of the shop. With the help of the large wheels, she had a sprightly step. I hoped that I might have the same lively pace when I turned her age. Little did I know the next change would put a big hitch in my stride.

* * *

"Entertainment!" Allison said, punching a fist in the air with excitement. "That's what the gallery needs."

With the continued rise of e-commerce, our customers' shopping habits continued to change. Customers wanted an experience they could delight in while shopping – something more enriching than just clicking on an item online.

Responding to the challenge, we created Candle-ology, a make-your-own candle experience, at the rear of our retail space. We offered a hundred scents to choose from, including Monkey's Breath, making kids giggle as the smell of bananas filled their noses. In no time, starting in 2013, Allison and her knack for trends and business had the candle department glowing.

Three years later, when she came to Larry and me saying that John had accepted a job 1,200 miles away in Colorado Springs, it snuffed out nearly all of my momentum.

As disheartening as the news was, in my heart I knew I had to celebrate their good fortune and encourage them to follow their dreams.

Deciding on a parting gift, I struggled with what to give Allison, with whom I had shared business, family, and just plain love of life for twenty-five years. Finally I decided to give her something that brought me the most joy. I painted a piece of art, focusing on one of my favorite times with her – traveling together on buying trips. Even though we had our share of travel snafus – bed bugs, fire drills, cancelled flights that forced us to drive 796 miles home – Allison's uplifting humor inspired me and kept me sane through it all.

Although I'm not known for portrait work, I carved out two figures in oil to represent us. I was delighted to be pushing myself in this figurative style. It seemed like the perfect way to honor Allison as she once again inspired me.

To this day, although we no longer work side-by-side, she continues to motivate me, as all my children and grandchildren do. With the ease of cell phone cameras and the instant sharing of photos, I feel closer to them. The enthusiasm of my family continues to ready me for life's never ending changes.

Chapter 58
Excited for More

The sun seeps brightly into the large storefront window of my art studio space in downtown Holland. It catches the shamrock-green oil paint on my palette. The vibrant color glows with energy, pulling my thoughts back to the present while I paint this canvas for my son, Adam. As the bright sunshine squirms through the branches of December's leafless locust tree and creates soft shadows on my palette, this high-in-the-sky sun tells me I have been lost in my thoughts for a while.

Suddenly the canvas becomes blurry. Tears pool in my eyes. I shake my head to pull myself out of the memories. Instead, my heart responds, tumbling and crashing, as I remember those early days of loneliness and struggle in that cracker-box Bismarck apartment, living alone. Naively, I never thought back then to question my unrealistic childhood expectations that someone else was responsible for my happiness.

Then, just as quickly, my heart comes alive to comfort me as I remind myself that I mustered up the courage to accept my weaknesses and forgive that younger and greener version of myself.

I take in a deep breath as I reassure myself. The zesty tang of oil paints and turpentine wrap me in comfort. Above my head, through the gallery speakers, I hear the smooth crooning of Brian McKnight's tenor voice floating through the air as a CD spins out the tunes during this holiday shopping season. The morning scurry of shoppers in the gallery is just beginning, but hearing the serene musical notes of "I'll Be *Home* for Christmas" keeps me focused on my thoughts.

Home. The word sings out crisp and clear. I am amazed how one word has a different, and powerful, meaning to each of us. For me, standing in front of Adam's canvas, I am reminded that I am at home with myself. I am happy. Even knowing that happiness is not a constant state in life, I am ready to keep going.

As I dip my knife into the thick paint on my palette and drag the green into the rich clear pigment of Thalo blue, the two colors ignite into a turquoise so explosive I can feel it. Excitement sends a spark to my heart. Like the birch tree I am presently painting, I unfurled my outer layer, accepted what is underneath, and kept growing, reaching upward toward my next dream. Whatever that may be.

Acknowledgements

I write in first person, but this project took many people to help me present my story with authenticity and, hopefully, grace.

My "coach" as I began to call her, Donna Stack, not only with this memoir but also with my other four books, has consistently been on Team Kate, reading *every* draft and revision. This is monumental. When I began writing my first book, *Beached in a Camper,* in 2009, I naïvely mixed past and present tense.

Others, too, have stayed with me from day one; Allison Dempkey and Mark Lewison, whose attention to detail allows me to soar.

Capturing the grass roots of my own personal story took additional help from memoir expert Lynn Lauber, also Dawn Dewitt-Brinks, Ann Staed, Maranda Shear, JoAnn Dornbos, Joy Eickelman, Allison Evans, Deb Evans, Lisa Denison, Robin Nichols, Kim TerHaar, Darcy TerHaar. I owe a special thank you to one of Wayne's relatives for input and blessing.

And, of course, without the support of my sons, Brian and Adam, my husband, Larry, and my mom, there would be no story.

Discussion Questions

1. How did Kate's mom and the era of the 1950s influence Kate? Have you had someone in your life that greatly influenced you?

2. Along Kate's journey, several friends inspired her to push forward. Do you have a favorite character whose words also inspired you?

3. Kate defines her joy by saying, "What joy to discover the complexity of watercolor! For the first time since I could remember I felt inspired and challenged and eager for more!" Can something specific and tangible define joy for you?

4. Was there something especially surprising about Kate's story? What was it and why?

5. What character traits does Kate possess that you wish you had? Why?

6. Kate uses the birch tree as her symbol to look within and to grow. Can you relate the birch to your own life?

7. Were there any lessons that you could take away from Kate's life story? What were they and why were they important?

Other Books by Kate Moynihan

Beached in a Camper: *Three weeks surviving an older brother, bug bites, water bombs, and a girl.*

Trouble Out West: *Six weeks surviving rattlesnakes, cowboy pranks, the ghost of General Custer, and the girls on the corner.*

Mystery in the Spooky Old House: *Brothers tackle hidden clues, sledding shenanigans, a sister with a secret, and a skater named Crusher.*

Available from Amazon.com, other retail outlets, and on Kindle.

Front Cover Art – *Summer*. One of the four seasons in our first Giclee print-on-demand series, 2003. "To this day, it is my favorite watercolor," Kate Moynihan.

Back Cover Art – *Early Morning*. Original oil, 2018. "My most treasured time of day," Kate Moynihan.

About Artist –
Author Kate Moynihan

Kate began her professional career as a registered nurse before branching out into the arts. Swinging a paintbrush will always be her creative roots, but she has grown to enjoy writing as well, starting with junior fiction novels about her two sons. Stretching her limbs, she embraces her journey in her memoir, *A Lone Birch*. In addition to being a gallery owner, Kate also enjoys public speaking, sharing the experiences of her multifaceted life. She lives in Holland, Michigan with her husband Larry where they will celebrate the 25th anniversary of Moynihan Gallery in May 2018.

Kate believes life could use a little delight. Her web site is bursting with it.

Visit: www.moynihangallery.com

Contact Kate: katemoynihan44@gmail.com or

Facebook: Kate Moynihan

Made in the USA
Monee, IL
06 July 2021

73018711R00174